FORGOTTEN AFRICA

Forgotten Africa introduces the general reader and beginning student to Africa's past, emphasizing those aspects only known or best known from archaeological and related evidence. It covers four million years of history across the continent, examining important aspects of Africa's momentous human story. The author is concerned to raise public awareness, both inside and outside Africa, to this frequently overlooked and often forgotten subject.

The 29 brief chapters look at human origins, the material culture of hunter-gatherers, the beginnings of African farming, the development of metallurgy, the emergence of distinctive artistic traditions, the growth of cities and states, the expansion of trading networks and the impact of European and other external contacts. The result is a fascinating and important story told in a straightforward and readable manner.

Graham Connah is currently a Visiting Fellow at the Australian National University, Canberra. He is the author of *Three Thousand Years in Africa*, *African Civilisations* and editor of *Transformations in Africa*. Graham Connah was awarded the Order of Australia in 2000.

FORGOTTEN AFRICA

An introduction to its archaeology

Graham Connah

Routledge
Taylor & Francis Group

LONDON AND NEW YORK

First published 2004
by Routledge
2 Park Square, Milton Park, Abingdon, Oxfordshire OX14 4RN

Simultaneously published in the USA and Canada
by Routledge
29 West 35th Street, New York, NY 10001

Routledge is an imprint of the Taylor & Francis Group

Typeset in Garamond by Wearset Ltd, Boldon, Tyne and Wear
Printed and bound in Great Britain by Antony Rowe Ltd,
Chippenham, Wiltshire

British Library Cataloguing in Publication Data
A catalogue record for this book is available from the British Library

Library of Congress Cataloging in Publication Data
Connah, Graham.
Forgotten Africa : an introduction to its archaeology / Graham
Connah.
p. cm.
Includes bibliographical references and index.
1. Africa–Antiquities. 2. Excavations (Archaeology)–Africa. I. Title.
DT13.C66 2004
960'.1–dc22
2004002073

ISBN 0-415-30590-X (hbk)
ISBN 0-415-30591-8 (pbk)
ISBN 0-203-51180-8 (ebook)

Dedicated to Charles Thurstan Shaw
One of the pioneers of African archaeology

CONTENTS

CONTENTS

ILLUSTRATIONS

PREFACE AND
ACKNOWLEDGEMENTS

This book is written by an archaeologist but it is not intended for other archaeologists as most archaeological writing appears to be. Instead, it is for a general readership and for those university students who need a brief introduction to the African past. For this reason, simplicity of presentation has been a major aim. For example, referencing has been limited to brief suggestions for further reading listed at the end of the book. Similarly, dating has been presented as years before the present, having in mind the variety of religious and cultural backgrounds amongst the readers that it is hoped to reach. In addition, a prose style has been adopted that is deliberately straightforward in its structure and in its vocabulary. This has also been done with possible future translators in mind, for any book about the African past deserves an audience wider than that of the English-speaking world alone. With this purpose of reaching out to those who wish to know about Africa's momentous past but find themselves discouraged by much of the available literature, the author's main objective has been to present the subject in an easily understood, readable and interesting form. Only the reader can decide whether this has been accomplished.

There are three major problems that must be faced when writing a book such as this. First, the subject is huge, over 4 million years of a whole continent. This has been tackled by an episodic rather than the usual narrative approach, resulting in a relatively large number of highly selective brief chapters, that are nevertheless ordered according to time and space. Second, much of the evidence, both archaeological and from a variety of other disciplines, is technically complex and often needs initial explanation if it is to be fully understood. This has not been attempted in this book, for there are many others that do it well. Instead, it is the conclusions from the available evidence rather than its variant methodologies that are the focus of attention here. Inevitably, this brings us to the third major problem, that of the often conflicting interpretations of that evidence. The general reader can be easily discouraged by the numerous disagreements amongst scholars that characterize the progress of research. Therefore, the approach adopted in this book has been to present those explanations that are currently most widely accepted, without frequent digressions into alternative views. The book was mostly written during 2003, although some parts of it originated as early as 2001. Although every effort was made to use the most up-to-date literature available, the difficulties in doing this should be appreciated.

It is a pleasure to acknowledge the help of many people who have assisted the author during the writing of this book. The advice and patience of Richard Stoneman and Celia Tedd at Routledge were particularly important. The generous hospitality of the School of Archaeology and Anthropology, at the Australian National University, Canberra, at which the author has been a Visiting Fellow in recent years, was also of assistance. Sue Singleton, of Umwelt Environmental Consultants, Toronto, New South Wales, produced the fourteen maps that form such an important part of the illustrations. She was greatly assisted in this work by Ian Kennedy. John Pratt, of the School of Art, at the Australian National University, drew Figures 3, 7 and 25. The sources of other illustrations are acknowledged in their captions, those without such acknowledgement being by the author. While every effort has been made to obtain permission to reproduce copyright items, in some cases, because of the passage of time or other circumstances, this has not been possible. The author and publishers would be glad to hear from any copyright holders not here acknowledged. As is apparent from the captions, colleagues as well as publishers and institutions were generous in their help with illustrative material. Thanks are especially due to David Phillipson but also to Christopher DeCorse, Gunnar Haaland, David Lewis-Williams, Rod McIntosh, Pierre de Maret, Julius Pistorius, Merrick Posnansky, Michael Rainsbury, Thurstan Shaw and Frank Willett. Others helped in a variety of ways, Sonja and Carlos Magnavita of the University of Frankfurt, for instance, spending time hunting out the nineteenth-century German publication that is the source of Figure 32. Similarly, Neal McCracken and Stuart Hay, photographers at the Australian National University, solved a variety of problems with some of the other illustrations. In addition, the author is grateful to Susan Fraser and Beryl Connah for reading the whole text and providing useful comments. Beryl Connah also compiled the Index. To all these people and to numerous others unnamed, the author extends his sincere thanks. Without their help the book would never have been completed. However, it would never have been even thought of without the support of countless people in Africa itself, with whom the author has come into contact during his many years of interest in their continent.

Graham Connah
School of Archaeology and Anthropology
Australian National University
Canberra
December 2003

Figure 1 Modern Africa as a guide to locations discussed in this book. Map by Sue Singleton.

1

AFRICA

The birthplace of humanity

It all began in Africa, for all of us. Many years of careful investigation by many researchers have shown that the remote origins of humanity can be traced only in the African continent. It has also been demonstrated that the genus *Homo*, to which we belong, emerged there at a much later time, and there is a strong likelihood that *Homo sapiens*, fully modern people like ourselves, also originated in Africa even later. Thus the three most important developments in the history of the world's most successful species took place in Africa. As one leading authority has remarked: we are all Africans under our skin. However, the African past has often been overlooked by historians, who have tended to concentrate on other parts of the world. Mainly, this has been because Africa's past has been largely a forgotten past, that has had to be painstakingly reconstructed because of a lack of written records in many areas until recent centuries. This reconstruction has been quite a late development, within the last 100 years and much of it within only the last 50 years. It has been based on evidence from a variety of sources, including the material remains of past human behaviour that archaeologists investigate and the remembered traditions of many African peoples. For the earliest periods, however, it is palaeontology, the study of fossil animal remains, and genetics, the study of inherited characteristics, that have been most important. They have provided the basic biological information that, together with the archaeological data, enable us to piece together the story of our origins, in Africa.

Fundamental to that task is the idea of evolution and the survival of the fittest, pioneered by Charles Darwin 150 years ago, and the work of geneticists who have explained the mechanism whereby characteristics are inherited and evolution takes place. To this must be added the success of geologists in establishing a framework for the earth's history and in discovering the environmental changes that occurred during that history. Working within that context, palaeontologists have been able to show how the fossil remains of life recovered from geological deposits demonstrate the process of evolution, as species continually adjusted to changing environments. The result was a succession of life forms of increasing complexity, that some 65 million years ago produced the earliest members of the zoological Order known as the Primates, to which humans as well as apes, monkeys and a number of other animals belong. Collectively, the apes and ourselves belong to the Superfamily known to zoologists as the Hominoidea but genetic evidence indicates that we have been separate from the apes for a long time. Our closest relative is the chimpanzee but, although we appear to have shared a common ancestor, we went our separate evolutionary ways between 5 and 8 million years ago. This is a period for which very little African fossil evidence is known, although there are fossils for earlier ape-like animals back to about 20 million years ago. The earliest evidence for the Hominoidae, the zoological Family to which we belong and whose members are usually referred to as hominids, is about 4.4 million years ago. It was then that our earliest recognizable ancestors stood up and began to walk upright.

Human palaeontologists, or palaeoanthropologists as they are often called, have classified our oldest ancestor in the genus *Australopithecus*, meaning 'southern ape', a name chosen because the first fossils to be identified were found in partly collapsed limestone caves in South Africa. However, australopithecines, as members of the genus are collectively called, have now also been found in sites stretching from Ethiopia to Malawi along the East African Rift Valley. With only one exception, they have not been found elsewhere in Africa and they are not known at all in other parts of the world. Their distribution within Africa suggests that they lived in an environment of tropical grassland and scattered trees, although sites containing their fossils are limited to geological deposits of relevant age which have been exposed by erosion or tectonic activity. Dating the evidence from such a remote period has been made possible by a range of techniques, of which radiopotassium dating, otherwise known as potassium/argon dating, is the most important for the East African sites. However, it is not applicable to the South African sites, which have mainly been dated by associated fauna that is also found in East African sites.

The first australopithecine of which substantial remains have been recovered is *Australopithecus afarensis*, known particularly from the Ethiopian site of Hadar and the Tanzanian site of Laetoli, the evidence at the latter place including a remarkable set of footprints preserved on an ancient surface. This hominid lived during the period from about 3.9 million to about 2.8 million years ago. It had a very small brain compared with modern people, around 415 cubic centimetres contrasting with the modern figure of about 1400 cubic centimetres. Its overall size was also small, males being about 151 centimetres in height and females only 105 centimetres. This difference between the sexes was also apparent in their relative weights, males weighing about 45 kilograms and females only 29 kilograms. The skull and dentition of *Australopithecus afarensis* reflected its essentially ape ancestry and the same impression is given by its powerful arms and short legs. It seems likely that although it could walk upright, it was also good at climbing trees.

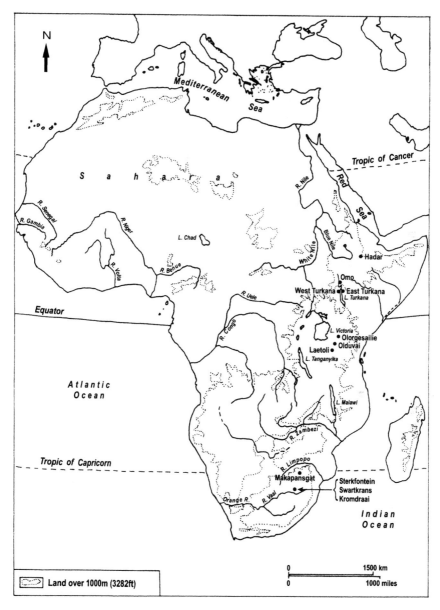

Figure 2 Sites with evidence for human origins. Refer to Chapters 1 and 2. Map by Sue Singleton.

Figure 3 An artist's impression of *Australopithecus afarensis*. John Pratt after Maurice Wilson in Andrews, P. and Stringer, C. 1989. *Human evolution: an illustrated guide*. British Museum (Natural History), London, Page 29.

The second of the better known australopithecines is *Australopithecus africanus*, the evidence for which comes from the South African cave sites, such as Sterkfontein and Makapansgat. It dates to between about 2.8 and about 2.3 million years ago and differed from *Australopithecus afarensis* in a number of ways. Most notably its brain size was a little larger, at around 440 cubic centimetres, and it had smaller front teeth and larger back teeth than its predecessor. However, its arms were longer than its legs, suggesting that it was still an efficient tree-climber as well as being able to walk upright. Although males remained larger than females, the difference was not quite so great as with *Australopithecus afarensis*. It seems likely that *Australopithecus africanus* had evolved from *Australopithecus afarensis* but both were small apelike creatures and the interpretation of the often fragmentary fossil evidence is made more difficult by the existence of several other australopithecine species.

Two of these were so different that, although generally regarded as australopithecines, they have been put into a separate genus by some authorities and given the name *Paranthropus*. This has been divided into the species *Paranthropus robustus* and *Paranthropus boisei*, the first found in the South African cave sites of Swartkrans and Kromdraai, the second found principally in the lowest deposits at Olduvai Gorge, in Tanzania, at East and West Turkana, in Kenya, and in the Omo Valley, in Ethiopia. Both species were characterized by extremely robust skulls, with massive back teeth, an enormous jaw, heavy cheekbones, and a bony crest on the top of the head. In tooth and jaw size they exceeded the largest male gorillas and it appears that the distinctive features of the skull were to enable great vertical force to be applied to the back teeth when eating. They existed during the same period, between about 2.3 and about 1 million years ago, differing from one another mainly in the extent to which they were robust, *Paranthropus boisei* being the more so. Indeed, because *Paranthropus boisei* has been found exclusively in East African sites and *Paranthropus robustus* only in South African sites, it is possible that they were simply geographical variants with a common ancestor. In spite of their appearance, these two species had a larger brain than other australopithecines, of about 520 cubic centimetres. Furthermore, although their heads were massively built, their bodies were remarkably small, the males being about 132–137 centimetres tall and weighing 40–49 kilograms, while the females were 110–124 centimetres in height and weighed 32–34 kilograms (*Paranthropus boisei* being the taller and heavier). Thus males remained noticeably larger than females, although perhaps a little less so than had been the case with the earlier hominids. Although undoubtedly able to walk upright, both species of *Paranthropus* had arms that suggest tree-climbing. However, so far as their place in human evolution is concerned, it appears that these species were a highly specialized branch that eventually died out, although existing at the same time as *Homo habilis*, the earliest member of the genus *Homo* (Chapter 2), and possibly longer. It was from *Homo habilis* that future hominids were to evolve and, although its ancestry remains controversial, it is possible that it was *Australopithecus africanus* rather than *Paranthropus* that was a part of it.

Reconstructing the behaviour of australopithecines is almost as difficult as deciding their evolutionary relationship to later hominids. This is because of the character of the evidence and the circumstances of its survival. It consists of skulls and other isolated bones or, more frequently, of fragments of these, and even partly complete skeletons are rare. In the case of the South

African cave sites the surviving pieces have been found mixed with animal bones in deposits cemented by lime and seem to be the leavings of predators such as hyenas and leopards. In the East African sites the fossil material has been preserved in lake or river sediments, into which it could have been washed sometime after death. In short, it is difficult to use such evidence to throw light on the lives of these early hominids. Even when possible living sites have been located, as at Olduvai Gorge, there have been the problems of separating the evidence for australopithecine behaviour from that relating to *Homo habilis*, that was also present, and of separating animal bones resulting from hunting from those left by animal predators. As a result, attempts to understand how the australopithecines lived have to be based mainly on inferences from the surviving skulls, teeth and other bones. Together with observations of modern chimpanzees and studies of recent hunter-gatherers, this approach makes it possible to gain some idea of what their life was like.

Judging from their fossil remains, australopithecines were as much at home in the trees as on the ground, suggesting that it was in the trees that they both sought refuge from predators and obtained some of their food. Indeed, most of what they ate probably came from plants, the massive back teeth of *Paranthropus* being most likely an adaptation to tough, hard vegetable materials. Some meat was probably also eaten but it is unclear whether this would have been obtained by actual hunting or by scavenging from animals that had died naturally or been killed by predators. Because males were so much larger than females, as with modern chimpanzees and other apes, it seems likely that australopithecine males similarly competed vigorously for females and that bonding between individual males and females did not occur. Furthermore, in spite of claims to the contrary, australopithecines do not seem to have fashioned stone tools, although they probably made use of sticks and stones in the ways that modern chimpanzees do. Finally, the shape of the base of australopithecine skulls is thought to indicate that these early hominids could not make the full range of sounds that modern people can and therefore had not developed language as we understand it. This would suggest that they were limited to the sort of noises by which modern chimpanzees communicate.

Australopithecines were small apelike creatures, whose small brains and physical characteristics suggest generally apelike behaviour. They seem not to have possessed the culture, that is to say the learned behaviour, of later hominids. Nevertheless, they were the apes that stood up and walked upright, possibly to aid food acquisition in an environment where grass was gradually replacing trees as climatic change occurred. As such, they are recognized as the earliest hominids and, although their evolutionary relationship to later hominids remains controversial, they appear to be our earliest ancestors. Paradoxically, it was with the appearance of these non-humans that humanity was born and it was born in Africa.

2

STONE TOOLS AND ADAPTATION

The origins of the genus *Homo*

Whatever the relationship of the australopithecines to ourselves, it is with the appearance of the earliest members of the genus *Homo*, to which we belong, that human evolution took a major leap forward. Important biological changes occurred and they were accompanied by the first indications of the human learned behaviour that anthropologists call culture. The strongest evidence for this new behaviour consists of the stone tools that were now made, probably for the first time. They demonstrate the existence of both greater manual dexterity and substantial mental development, to which their manufacture must also have contributed. Their possession enabled their makers to adapt to a greater range of environments and, almost certainly, to increase the meat content of their diet. Stone tools could also have contributed to a more efficient exploitation of plant foods and made it possible to shape wood and use animal skins. The earliest of such tools were simple and persisted from about 2.6–2.5 million years ago to about 1.7–1.6 million years ago. However, more sophisticated forms were subsequently developed and were made until about 250,000 years ago, by which time further evolutionary changes had occurred amongst their makers. Furthermore, by sometime before 1 million years ago early humans had not only spread into most African environments but had also expanded beyond the continent. Crucial to that achievement was the interaction of culture and evolution that characterized this long period.

The earliest member of the genus *Homo* is represented by fossils that have been named *Homo habilis*, meaning 'handy man'. These are best known from deposits dated to roughly 1.9–1.8 million years ago at Olduvai Gorge, in Tanzania, and East Turkana, in Kenya. However, other finds from Ethiopia, Kenya and Malawi indicate that *Homo habilis* emerged much earlier, perhaps about 2.5–2.4 million years ago. Its most distinctive feature was a brain that was larger than those of the australopithecines, being of about 630 cubic centimetres. In addition, the back teeth were smaller, although not in all specimens and it is uncertain whether this is just a difference between the sexes or an indication that more than one species was present. In spite of the increased skull size, bodies remained small, but larger for males than for females, the former being about 157 centimetres high and about 52 kilograms in weight, compared with females of about 125 centimetres and about 32 kilograms. Arms that were relatively long compared with the legs, suggest that *Homo habilis* retained the tree-climbing ability of its predecessors, as well as being fully capable of walking upright. Nevertheless, this early species of *Homo* does appear to represent an important stage in evolutionary development, for not only was the brain larger but there are indications that its structure was more like that of later humans and less like that of previous australopithecines. It is possible that this means that there was a developing capacity for speech.

Whether or not this was the case, *Homo habilis* certainly demonstrated an ability to make stone tools. Although this hominid coexisted with *Paranthropus* (Chapter 1) for perhaps a million years, it seems that such tools were not produced by the latter. These 'stone artefacts', as archaeologists prefer to call them, were simple by later standards, consisting of flakes and the cores from which they were struck, as well as hammerstones. However, the flakes could have been put to a variety of uses, such as working wood, cutting up meat and scraping hide, the cores could also have functioned as choppers, and the hammerstones probably served both to strike flakes from cores and to smash animal bones in order to extract their marrow or to crack nuts. Collectively these earliest stone artefacts are known as the Oldowan Industrial Complex, after Olduvai Gorge where they were first studied in detail. Their manufacture represents a marked departure from previous early hominid behaviour, particularly because they have been found together with fragmentary animal bones at some sites, including Olduvai Gorge and East Turkana. These places have provided the first evidence for human behaviour other than that derived from the anatomy of the fossils. Variously described as living sites or butchery sites, their interpretation is controversial because of indications that animal predators were also active at such sites but they do suggest that *Homo habilis* was consuming more meat than earlier or less evolved hominids. Whether it was obtained by scavenging from carnivore kills or from actual hunting is uncertain but it does appear that it was being obtained, and stone tools were making this easier than before.

Approximately 1.8–1.7 million years ago there appeared an even more advanced hominid, which has been named *Homo ergaster* and which existed until perhaps 600,000 years ago. It had probably evolved from *Homo habilis* or one of its variants. Fossils of *Homo ergaster* have been found at Olduvai Gorge, East and West Turkana, and Swartkrans, in South Africa, as well as at sites in Uganda, Ethiopia and Eritrea. Indicative of the success of this species, possibly relevant fossils have also been found far to the north in both Morocco and Algeria. It differed from its predecessors principally by having a much enlarged brain of about 907 cubic centimetres. However, much of this increase might relate to a greater body size, particularly for females, *Homo ergaster* being the first hominid for which stature and weight were approximately that of modern people and where the difference between males and females was about the same as at present. Nevertheless, the shape of the skull suggests that some reorganization of the brain accompanied its increase in size, although a massive brow ridge would have given the face an apelike appearance. These possible changes in the brain suggest that *Homo ergaster* could have been the first hominid to possess rudimentary language. In addition, this species was characterized by a further reduction in the size of its back teeth and by arms and legs that indicate that it relied totally on upright walking and no longer combined it with tree-climbing as earlier hominids had done. Taking all these changes into consideration, it is probably reasonable to regard *Homo ergaster* as the first true human species.

Not only does the anatomical evidence support such a claim, cultural evidence also supports it. At about the same time that *Homo ergaster* appeared, stone artefacts also became more sophisticated. Cutting tools were now flaked on both sides in order to produce a sharp edge. Archaeologists call these 'bifaces' and the examples which are thought to have been made

0   5   10
cm

Figure 4 Stone tools of *Homo ergaster*. Left, a hand-axe, right, a cleaver, both from Bed III, Olduvai Gorge, Tanzania. Reproduced by permission of Cambridge University Museum of Archaeology and Anthropology, accession numbers: (hand-axe) CUMAA 1934.1107B and (cleaver) CUMAA 1934.1107A.

by *Homo ergaster* are regarded as belonging to the Acheulean Industrial Tradition, named after a site in France. Most distinctive were pointed leaf-shaped bifaces known to archaeologists as 'hand-axes', although this name gives a misleading idea of their probable use. Their cutting edge usually extended around two sides but other bifaces, known more appropriately as 'cleavers', had a transverse cutting edge instead of a point. These Acheulean tools seem to have developed from the preceding Oldowan artefacts and the latter continued to be made alongside the new types. This provided *Homo ergaster* with a more effective tool-kit than previously available, making it possible to exploit the resources of a wide range of environments. Consequently, sites with assemblages of Acheulean artefacts have been found from South Africa to Ethiopia and from Ethiopia to North West Africa, although they are less well known in West and Central Africa. The production of these tools, particularly of the often beautifully made bifaces, is a clear indication of both manual skill and the mental ability to plan a series of manufacturing stages. Modern archaeologists who have successfully made bifaces during their experiments have found that the process requires to be carefully learned. By one means or another, it seems that *Homo ergaster* and some succeeding early humans were able to pass on such knowledge for about 1.5 million years.

The stone artefacts made by *Homo ergaster* seem to have been put to a variety of uses, including the butchery of animals that had been hunted or scavenged. The bifaces might have been particularly useful for cutting up carcasses, although sharp flakes were also probably employed. Numerous sites have been found where Acheulean artefacts and sometimes broken animal bones appear to mark the location of such activity or of actual living sites. Most seem to have been located near water and some consist of quite remarkable collections of material. One that has been studied in detail is the site of Olorgesailie, in the Kenyan Rift Valley, where several large concentrations of hand-axes, cleavers and other stone artefacts occur in an area that was at the side of a small lake. Although some movement of the material due to subsequent water action is likely, its distribution and the presence of broken animal bone at some locations, suggest that early humans intermittently camped at this place over a very long period. As with earlier evidence of this sort, it is difficult to assess how much animal predators might have contributed to the fragmented bone and it is likely that plant food, of which evidence has not survived, was also important. Furthermore, neither living structures nor evidence of fire-use can be identified with certainty at Olorgesailie. Nevertheless, the large number of artefacts present and indications that a tonne or more of stones suitable for their manufacture had been carried to the site from several kilometres away, suggest its repeated use as some sort of home base. *Homo ergaster* no longer showed the great difference in size between males and females evident amongst earlier hominids. This could indicate that competition between males for access to females had

Figure 5 Olorgesailie, in the Kenyan Rift Valley: a dense scatter of stone artefacts made by *Homo ergaster*. The modern walkway and roofed structure are to protect the site.

become less vigorous and that pair-bonding was developing, with consequences for the social groups that visited such places as Olorgesailie.

One of the clearest indications of the successful adaptation of *Homo ergaster* to a variety of environments is the way that it expanded out of Africa, in the form of its evolutionary successor *Homo erectus*. This appears to have happened sometime before 1 million years ago and at the important site of Zhoukoudian, far away in northern China, *Homo erectus* was present between about 500,000 and 240,000 years ago. Perhaps by an even earlier time it had also reached the island of Java in South-East Asia and there is evidence for its presence in Europe by 600,000–500,000 years ago and possibly before that. *Homo erectus* was sufficiently similar to *Homo ergaster* for some authorities to place them both in the *erectus* species but the latter did differ in some respects, most notably in its brain size which was generally of more than 1000 cubic centimetres. However, concerning the interpretation of the relevant fossil evidence from Asia and Europe there is some controversy, particularly on the subject of dating. There is also a problem with the stone artefacts, that are of course much more common than the fossils. This is because the Acheulean Industrial Tradition is found in western Asia and western Europe, just as it is found in Africa, but in eastern Asia and possibly extending westwards across south-central Asia to eastern Europe, the stone artefacts belong instead to what is known as the chopper-chopping tool

11

complex. Clearly, these difficulties will not be resolved until a great deal more evidence is available for study.

The appearance of the earliest members of the genus *Homo* was an evolutionary development of fundamental importance for the later history of humankind. Anatomical changes in *Homo habilis, Homo ergaster and Homo erectus*, compared with the australopithecines, were of the greatest significance, particularly in respect of the enlargement and possible restructuring of the brain. These changes seem to have resulted in the gradual emergence of a distinctively human culture, of which the manufacture of stone tools is the principal surviving evidence, and which in turn stimulated further evolutionary change. The result was an increasing capacity to adapt to a wide variety of environments, that enabled early humans not only to spread through most of Africa but also to expand into the wider world.

3

AFRICA'S GIFT TO THE WORLD

The earliest *Homo sapiens*

The interpretation of the often fragmentary evidence for human evolution inevitably causes disagreement and controversy. Not surprisingly, this has been particularly the case regarding the immediate origins of our own species of anatomically modern humans, *Homo sapiens*. It is apparent that in Europe and western Asia the continuing evolutionary process eventually led to a highly specialized hominid, *Homo neanderthalensis*, so-called 'Neanderthal Man', whose relationship to later humans has been the subject of much debate. Current thinking tends to regard it as an aberrant offshoot, adapted to the cold of the Eurasian 'Ice Ages', that was replaced by fully modern humans 50,000–40,000 years ago. The latter, it is thought, came from Africa, where the earliest members of *Homo sapiens* had evolved after about 600,000 years ago and where *Homo neanderthalensis* was absent. In eastern Asia, however, a lack of sufficient evidence for the relevant period makes interpretation even more difficult and it is uncertain whether later *Homo erectus* evolved into *Homo sapiens* independently or was replaced by or interbred with the latter spreading out from Africa. The most favoured explanation at present is that all *Homo sapiens* ultimately derived from Africa, reaching even Australia by about 40,000 years ago. Thus it appears that the earliest members of our species could well have been Africa's gift to the world.

The evidence supporting this theory consists of African fossil skulls and other bones that have been attributed to early forms of *Homo sapiens* or to its close relatives. One of the best known and earliest examples is a nearly complete skull from Broken Hill (also known as Kabwe), in Zambia. Dating perhaps from about 400,000 years ago, this individual had a brain of 1285 cubic centimetres and a skull that was more rounded in some areas than its predecessors. Also relevant are skulls from Elandsfontein, in South Africa, Jebel Irhoud, in Morocco, Singa, in the Sudan, and several other places, which have been variously dated to between 600,000 and 90,000 years ago but mostly to the second half of this period. Collectively, they begin to show features characteristic of our own species but without those characteristic of *Homo neanderthalensis*, that gradually developed in Europe and western Asia

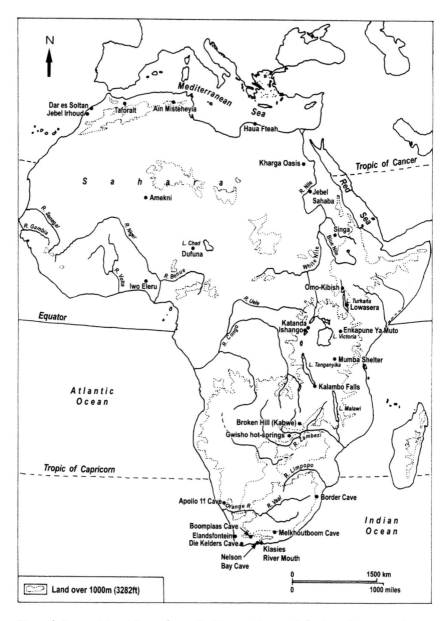

Figure 6 Sites with evidence for early *Homo sapiens* and for later hunter-gatherers. Refer to Chapters 3 and 4. Map by Sue Singleton.

Figure 7 An artist's impression of early *Homo sapiens*, based on the skull from Broken Hill (Kabwe) in Zambia. John Pratt after Maurice Wilson in Andrews, P. and Stringer, C. 1989. *Human evolution: an illustrated guide*. British Museum (Natural History), London, Page 41.

and was dominant from about 127,000 to 50,000–40,000 years ago. It seems most likely, therefore, that the earliest African *Homo sapiens* evolved from *Homo ergaster* within Africa itself, separate from developments in Europe. By the Neanderthal period Africa appears to have been occupied by people who were anatomically much like ourselves, of whom fossil evidence has been found at many places. Some idea of geographical distribution and dating can be gained from a selection of the major sites. Klasies River Mouth, in South Africa, produced material from between 115,000 and 60,000 years ago; Border Cave, in South Africa, from between 90,000 and 50,000 years ago; and Die Kelders Cave 1, also in South Africa, from between 71,000 and 45,000 years ago. Further north, Mumba Shelter, in Tanzania, produced material from between 130,000 and 109,000 years ago; Omo-Kibish, in Ethiopia, from between 127,000 and 37,000 years ago; and Dar es Soltan Cave 2, in Morocco, possibly from between 127,000 and

40,000 years ago. Similar near-modern human material has also been found in Israel, which is almost an extension of the African continent, dated to between 120,000 and 80,000 years ago. Thus there is abundant fossil evidence for the African origin of *Homo sapiens*.

Cultural evidence is much more common than fossil evidence during this long period and suggests increasingly human behaviour compared with earlier times. For instance, large numbers of stone artefacts have been found, many of which indicate greater technological sophistication than previously. The changes that took place are difficult to define but in general the large bifaces of the Acheulean (Chapter 2) disappeared and stone artefacts became dominated by flakes, some of which were of the long, narrow form known to archaeologists as 'blades'. At times these were struck from cores that had already been flaked to determine the shape and size of the piece that was removed. This is called the Levallois technique, after a site in France, and seems to have been already used in Africa during the late Acheulean period. Some of the flakes and blades were also shaped by further flaking, resulting in a range of scrapers, points, notched pieces, borers and other tools. In such matters, many African stone industries of this period loosely resembled those of contemporary Europe but there was also considerable regional diversity resulting in quite distinctive African forms. For example, in the northwest of Africa Aterian points and other flake tools had carefully worked tangs, so that they could be fixed to shafts or handles, and in much of central and western Africa large core tools continued to be made such as those known as Sangoan 'picks'. Perhaps most remarkable was the production of very small blades with blunted backs in the Howieson's Poort industry of South Africa, around 70,000 years ago. Such 'microliths', as they are known to archaeologists, were to be one of the characteristic artefacts of later hunter-gatherers but in the Howieson's Poort industry they appeared much earlier than elsewhere in Africa or even the rest of the world.

The wide range of stone tools that was made by early *Homo sapiens* in Africa indicates an increased capacity to exploit surrounding environments and, indeed, the people of this period seem to have occupied almost every corner of the continent. This might suggest that populations were increasing but they probably remained very small, as well as being subject to environmental fluctuations such as those that at times rendered the Sahara uninhabitable. However, our knowledge of human behaviour is better for this period than for earlier ones, because from this time onwards evidence was often preserved in cave deposits. Earlier evidence is so old that caves have usually collapsed or eroded away and we are mostly limited to information from open sites buried in lake or river sediments. In contrast, it now also becomes possible to investigate sites that are confined within a cave or under an overhang of rock and which provided intermittent shelter for human occupants sometimes for very long periods. Many of these sites have been highly informative about the lives of the earliest members of our

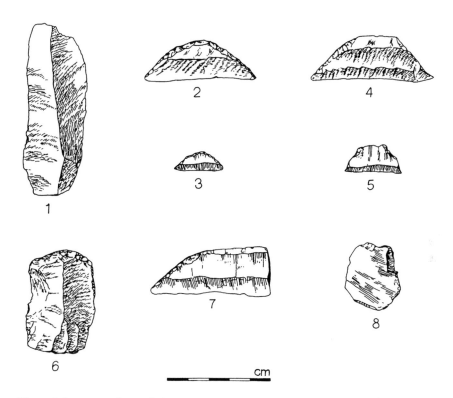

Figure 8 Stone artefacts of the Howieson's Poort industry, Klasies River Mouth, South Africa. 1. Blade. 2–5 and 7. Microliths with blunted backs. 6. End-scraper. 8. Burin. After selections from Singer, R. and Wymer, J. 1982. *The Middle Stone Age at Klasies River Mouth in South Africa.* University of Chicago Press, Chicago and London, Figures 6.2–6.5.

species, yielding evidence for hunting and the use of fire, as well as large numbers of stone tools, and enabling the study of changes in human activities as time passed. When considered in conjunction with information that continues to be provided by open sites, a fuller understanding of this period can be achieved than of any previous one. Two cave sites, at opposite ends of the African continent, and one open site at its centre, are outstanding examples.

The first of these is the cave complex at Klasies River Mouth, on the south coast of South Africa. This remarkable site has archaeological and natural deposits more than 18 metres deep, that accumulated from about 120,000 to about 1000 years ago and which contain a stratified sequence of stone artefacts. The site also contains hearths, showing that it was a favoured living place, the resources of both land and sea being accessible and with plentiful freshwater nearby. Klasies River Mouth was one of the sources of early *Homo sapiens* remains and also provided some of the evidence for the Howieson's Poort industry of about 70,000 years ago. The latter constituted an interruption in the Klassies River sequence, that otherwise consisted of industries of parallel-sided and pointed flakes and blades. A few of these were shaped by further flaking, or 'retouched' to use the archaeological term, to produce spear-points that were presumably hafted, as well as scrapers and chisel-like tools called 'burins'. These flake and blade industries continued at Klasies River for a very long time, perhaps for as much as about 80,000 years, except for the Howieson's Poort interruption. They were made by people who exploited both land and marine animals for food, and who collected shellfish but rarely fished. Cut-marks on some of the animal bones found in the site show that hunting was practised, initially with a preference for large animals such as eland and buffalo and later for smaller antelope. The African buffalo is a cunning and ferocious animal, so that it must have taken courage to attack it with a stone-tipped spear and, not surprisingly, many of those killed were very young. However, it does appear that the Klasies River people were hunting not merely scavenging; one buffalo verte-bra from the site still had the tip of a stone point embedded in it. The Howieson's Poort interlude seems to represent a time when spears barbed with microliths and possibly even bows and microlith-barbed arrows were used to hunt the smaller antelope. Nevertheless, the flake and blade indus-tries subsequently reappeared, until the sea fell below its present level and receded from the site, which was effectively abandoned for perhaps about 50,000 years until reoccupied about 3000 years ago.

The second site is the great cave of Haua Fteah, on the north coast of North Africa, situated in what is now Libya. Here again there are deep deposits, in this case more than 13 metres in depth but their base has never been reached by excavation. Again they present an important sequence of stone industries, at this site extending from perhaps 70,000 years ago to historical times. The oldest known of these consisted of heavy blades and flakes, some of which were retouched to produce scrapers and burins. The animal bones from the site indicated that the makers of these stone tools hunted wild cattle, gazelle, zebra and Barbary sheep, as well as collecting snails and, because the cave was at that time near the coast, exploiting shell-fish. Their stone industry was made for at least 5000 years, being eventually replaced by a second flake and blade industry that lasted for over 20,000 years until about 40,000 years ago, when it in turn was replaced by a more developed blade industry more recent than the time-span of this chapter. Associated with the second industry were parts of two human jaws of anatomically modern people. Finally, as at Klasies River Mouth, in spite of the numerous animal bones that were recovered from the deposits, there was no convincing use of bone as a raw material, a practice that was to be charac-teristic of later hunter-gatherers (Chapter 4).

The third place to be considered is Kalambo Falls, in northern Zambia.

Here a number of open sites have been found in sediments built up by an intermittent lake above the 220-metre-high waterfall. Yet again, deep deposits have provided a long cultural sequence, in this case stretching from the Acheulean period right on to recent centuries, although the lowest levels could not be reached because of water. The sequence is relevant to this discussion because it includes stratified Sangoan stone artefacts, perhaps dating from about 100,000 to about 80,000 years ago, as well as other artefacts that are a little later. Some of the Sangoan artefacts were interpreted as representing a living site, a most significant discovery because artefacts of this type have been found so rarely in such a context. However, because bone is not preserved at Kalambo, there is no evidence for the subsistence economy of those who occupied the site. Therefore, important though the Kalambo Falls sites are, particularly for understanding the evolution of stone-working technology, they demonstrate the exceptional value of major cave sites, where enclosed environments usually preserve a greater range of evidence for human behaviour.

It is Africa that provides the fossil evidence for the origin and evolution of the earliest members of our species, *Homo sapiens*. It also provides contemporary archaeological evidence for increasingly human behaviour, that eventually enabled hunter-gatherers to exploit almost every environment in the continent. Indeed, it seems that by 50,000–40,000 years ago African hunter-gatherers were ready to take on the world, and that, if the most widely accepted theory is correct, is what they proceeded to do.

4

LIVING OFF THE LAND

Later hunter-gatherers in Africa

By 50,000–40,000 years ago, if not earlier, Africa was inhabited by fully modern people, so that the archaeological evidence for their behaviour becomes more important than the evidence for anatomical change. They lived by hunting and gathering, the longest-lasting of human economies, but their exploitation of environments appears to have become more intense than that of their predecessors. This can be seen in their use of raw materials, in their acquisition of food, and in the variety of their adaptations. Along with this increased efficiency, there was an emerging awareness of themselves and their place in the world. Such is indicated by evidence for personal adornment, the formal burial of the dead and the practice of art. There are also signs of violence between people, probably brought about by competition for resources. In short, the later hunter-gatherers of Africa have left archaeological evidence for many aspects of modern human behaviour. Furthermore, because small groups of them survived until recent times, such as the San people of the Kalahari Desert, it is possible to use ethnographic observations to set the archaeological evidence in a broader context, that helps to explain how people were able to live off the land for so long. However, many later hunter-gatherers in Africa must have innovated in order to survive, because it was they who were responsible for the changes that after about 10,000 years ago led to the production rather than the collection of food (Chapters 7 and 8).

The most plentiful archaeological evidence for African later hunter-gatherers remains stone artefacts. Characteristically, these are in the form of microliths, very small flakes or blades with blunted backs, that formed the cutting components of composite tools. Often only 1–2 centimetres in length, these tiny sharp pieces of stone were mounted on spears and arrows, to form barbs and points, or in handles to provide the edges of knives and other tools. Grooves in the wood or bone shafts and handles aided this process and vegetable resins were used to cement the microliths in place. This might seem a crude technology compared with some earlier stone-working but it was actually much more efficient. For instance, the manufacture of microliths produced a greater total length of cutting edge per

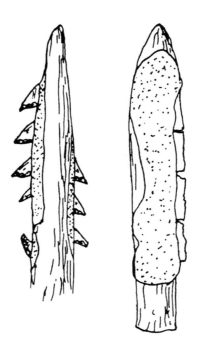

Figure 9 How some microliths were used: left, as barbs on the head of a wooden spear or arrow; right, as the cutting edge of a knife with a wooden handle. Stippled areas represent vegetable resin. Reproduced by permission of the publishers from Clark, J.D. 1970. *The prehistory of Africa*. Thames and Hudson, London, Figure 43.

kilogram of raw material than either core tools or large flake tools. Because stone suitable for flaking was not always easy to obtain and in some instances had to be carried some distance, this was a decided advantage. In addition, microliths were 'throw-away' artefacts. Like many things in modern life, if they were lost or broken or worn out, they could be easily replaced. Stone artefacts of this sort were already being made by about 46,000 years ago, according to evidence from the Kenyan rockshelter of Enkapune Ya Muto, and they also occurred as early as about 70,000 years ago in the South African Howieson's Poort industry (Chapter 3). After roughly 15,000–10,000 years ago they became widely used in Africa, for example in the Capsian industry of North Africa, the Nachikufan industry of Zambia, and the Wilton industry of South Africa. However, some larger stone tools continued to be made, including core tools in some areas, and percussion, grinding and drilling began to be used for shaping stone axes, grindstones and bored stones.

The manufacture of microliths meant that the choice of raw material could be more selective than formerly, because less was needed. Greater use could be made of finer-grained stones that were relatively uncommon and usually available only in small pieces. Another important change in raw material was the use of bone for the production of artefacts, a practice that was previously rare. For instance, by about 10,000 years ago at Nelson Bay Cave, South Africa, there were bone points, spatulate tools and double-pointed bone slivers that were used like fish hooks. Most remarkable, however, are the numerous barbed bone points that have been found at sites widely distributed in the Sahara Desert, the Sahel, the Nile Valley, and amongst the East African lakes. Some of these were apparently intended to be fixed to the end of a spear or arrow shaft but many seem to have been harpoon heads, that would have separated from their shaft on impact but remained attached to it by a line. Both types are often beautifully carved, usually with either one or two rows of barbs and often with a grooved butt, suitable for binding to a shaft, or a notch or perforation for the attachment of a retention line. They were made principally from about 10,000 to about 1000 years ago but barbed bone points from the site of Ishango, on the shores of Lake Edward in Democratic Congo, are thought to date from about 20,000 years ago. Indeed, examples from the nearby site of Katanda have been dated to 90,000 years ago, although this date has been questioned.

A raw material with importance for the future was fired clay, which later hunter-gatherers were the first to use for the manufacture of containers, thus producing the first African pottery. The earliest of this seems to have been made in the Sahara, occurring for instance at Amekni, in southern Algeria, between about 9500 and about 8500 years ago. Perhaps slightly later it also appeared in the middle Nile Valley and in parts of East Africa, and by 2000 years ago pottery was even being made by hunter-gatherers in the far south of South Africa. Archaeologists used to think that early farming societies invented pottery but this appears not to have been the case. It most likely resulted from hunter-gatherer requirements for food preparation, particularly of some of the tougher plant foods which cooking in a pot would have made more edible. The appearance of pottery in some areas suggests that its makers were becoming at least semi-sedentary: heavy and fragile pots would have been unsuitable for a highly nomadic way of life.

Occasionally, later hunter-gatherer sites also reveal the use of other materials, that previously left little or no direct evidence in spite of their probable importance. This occurs when there is unusually good preservation, as in the dry deposits of Melkhoutboom Cave in South Africa, which produced substantial organic remains some of which are more than 6000 years old. These included wooden artefacts, such as pegs and fire-drills, as well as parts of reed arrow shafts and the remains of plant foods. There were also items of leather, some of which had been sewn, including part of a man's loin cloth. In addition, there were fragments of string and netting made from vegetable fibre. In contrasting conditions, at Gwisho hot-springs in Zambia, wet deposits also yielded an impressive collection of organic mater-

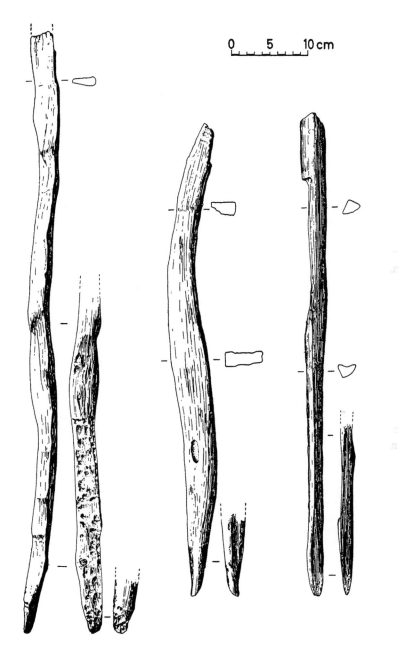

Figure 10 Three wooden digging sticks from Gwisho hot-springs, in Zambia. Reproduced by permission of the Prehistoric Society from Fagan, B.M. and Van Noten, F.L. 1966. Wooden implements from Late Stone Age sites at Gwisho hot-springs, Lochinvar, Zambia. *Proceedings of the Prehistoric Society*, New Series 32, part of Figure 4.

ial, in this case from about 4000 years ago. Several wooden digging sticks, wooden arrowheads, and other pieces of worked wood were found. There were also large quantities of reeds and grass, that might have been the remains of mats. Organic remains, such as those from Melkhoutboom and Gwisho, are a powerful reminder of the variety of evidence for human behaviour which usually has not survived from so long ago. An outstanding example of this is the dugout canoe, dated to about 8000 years ago, found at Dufuna in the north-east of Nigeria (Chapter 14).

The stone, bone, pottery, wooden and leather artefacts, together with the plant remains, suggest that later hunter-gatherers were exploiting a more varied resource base than their predecessors. Some of the microliths were probably mounted as points and barbs on arrows, and the reed arrow shafts from Melkhoutboom and the wooden arrowheads from Gwisho indicate that the bow and arrow had already come into use. In Africa this probably happened by about 20,000 years ago and would have made the hunting of birds and fast-moving smaller animals easier than before. In addition, the double-pointed bone slivers and the barbed bone points indicate the development of fishing, previously rare or absent. So do the numerous fish bones that are found at many later hunter-gatherer sites, often together with barbed points. Furthermore, many later sites have grindstones that were probably used for the preparation of some of the plant foods that were consumed, particularly wild grass seeds, although they could also have served other purposes. The harvesting of wild grasses is further suggested by the existence of a characteristic polish on those microliths that probably formed the cutting edges of sickles. The possession of bored stones with which to weight digging sticks and of ground-edge axes, that probably had many uses, also indicates an increasing capacity to exploit the environment. Thus the later hunter-gatherer period in Africa can be seen as one of overall intensification, when changes gradually occurred that in some places were to culminate in the herding of animals and the cultivation of plants.

Intensification is also indicated by the variety of later hunter-gatherer adaptations. People lived in the open, in shelters or huts, as well as occupying rock shelters and caves, many of them moving seasonally in order to exploit resources as they became available. A wide range of strategies made it possible to inhabit almost every environment. For instance, people at the Algerian site of Aïn Misteheyia, between about 9500 and about 6500 years ago, supplemented their diet in their semi-arid environment by eating large numbers of land snails. At a roughly similar date, people in the eastern Sahara were apparently harvesting wild cereals at Kharga Oasis. In contrast, later hunter-gatherers at Iwo Eleru, in southern Nigeria, were exploiting the rainforest or its margins by 12,000 years ago, and in East Africa, at Lowasera on Lake Turkana, others were using barbed bone points to catch fish by about 9000 years ago. In South Africa, between about 8000 and about 4000 years ago, people at Boomplaas Cave were relying on the hunting of small browsing antelope, and at Nelson Bay Cave, between about 4000 and about 2000 years ago, the most common mammals hunted were seals and hyraxes. These examples give some idea of the many different ways in which later hunter-gatherers were able to exploit so many different environments.

Perhaps the most significant aspect of modern human behaviour amongst later hunter-gatherers in Africa concerns their ideas about themselves and

Figure 11 Burial of two adult males in the cemetery at Jebel Sahaba, Sudan. A total of 25 microliths were found with this burial, including two embedded in the bones of one of the individuals, suggesting that the microliths were the points and barbs of projectiles which were the cause of death. From Clark, J.D. 1970. *The prehistory of Africa.* Thames and Hudson, London, Plate 35 (source: F. Wendorf).

their world. Thus it is this period that has produced the earliest clear evidence in Africa for the use of items of personal adornment. Small disc-shaped beads made by drilling and grinding pieces of ostrich eggshell appeared as early as about 40,000 years ago at the Kenyan site of Enkapune Ya Muto and from then on remained an important item of both decoration and exchange. Furthermore, it was later hunter-gatherers who were responsible for the earliest formal burials in Africa, which have been found, for instance, from about 16,000 years ago at Taforalt, in Morocco. Indeed, at Jebel Sahaba in the Sudan, a number of burials that date to 14,000–12,000 years ago were of people who had died violently, indicating the antiquity of another aspect of modern human behaviour. Finally, later hunter-gatherers also produced Africa's earliest art, naturalistic paintings of animals on loose stone slabs being dated to about 26,000 years ago at Apollo 11 Cave in Namibia. The more numerous later rock paintings and engravings provide important insights into both the material and spiritual life of the people who produced them (Chapters 5 and 6).

In South Africa and parts of East and Central Africa some hunter-gatherers continued to live in basically the same way until modern times, so that researchers have been able to observe their activities and talk to them. This has helped considerably in the task of interpreting the archaeological evidence for Africa's later hunter-gatherers. In addition, many farming people in Africa have continued to hunt and fish, in order to supplement their diet, and particularly during periods of famine they have been known to collect wild plants as food. It is therefore apparent that the line between hunter-gathering and farming is less certain than used to be thought. It seems that some later hunter-gatherers eventually gained sufficient control over their resources to be able to produce rather than collect food. In a sense, it was their success that in most areas brought an end to their way of living.

5

PUTTING IDEAS ON STONE
The rock art of southern Africa

It was later hunter-gatherers who produced Africa's first art. Subsequently, both they and early farmers were responsible for large numbers of paintings and engravings, that have survived on rock surfaces in many parts of the continent. However, it is the rock art of the Sahara and that of southern Africa that have been most intensively studied, because they are potentially the most informative. Both provide documents of forgotten lives but they are documents that are both difficult to date and to read. The southern African art not only started first but was practised for a longer time, so that some of the last of the people whose artists were responsible for it could be asked about its meaning. In the case of the Saharan art (Chapter 6) this was not possible, making its interpretation more difficult, but even the rock art of southern Africa has been the subject of much discussion regarding its purpose. At one time some archaeologists assumed that the paintings and engravings were merely done for pleasure, others suggesting that they represented hunting magic, depiction of an animal enabling the hunter subsequently to kill it. More recently it has been argued that this art actually expresses complex ideas of fundamental importance to the society that produced it. For that society it was a means of communication and a source of power. Just as modern people put ideas on paper, the later hunter-gatherers of southern Africa put them on stone.

Rock art has been found in many parts of southern Africa, defining that region as consisting of the modern states of Namibia, Botswana and South Africa. The most noticeable characteristic of its distribution is that the paintings are found principally in rock shelters amongst the mountains at the edge of the southern African plateau but the engravings are restricted to the semi-arid plains of the interior, where rock shelters are rare. In spite of some differences between these art forms, they have enough in common to suggest that they were the work of people with similar ideas. This is also the case amongst the paintings themselves, where three main groups can be identified. These are, first, Namibia and the western Cape; second, the central plateau; and third, the eastern Cape and the south-eastern mountains. Large numbers of particularly impressive paintings exist in the

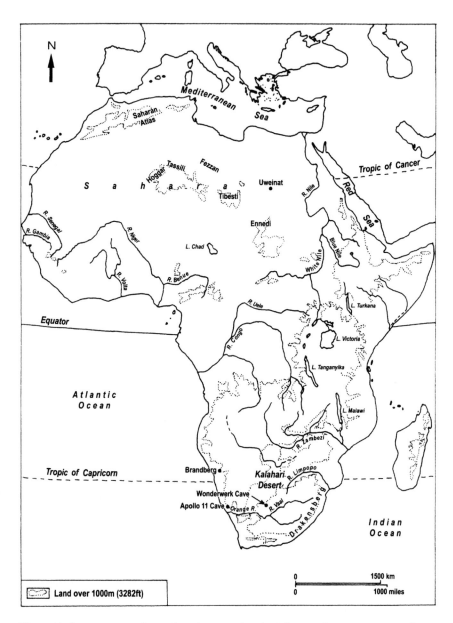

Figure 12 Important rock art locations in South Africa and the Sahara. Refer to Chapters 5 and 6. Map by Sue Singleton.

Brandberg area of the first of these groups and in the Drakensberg mountains of the third group. Most of the art, whether engraved or painted and whichever group to which it belongs, was the work of Khoisan-speaking hunter-gatherers, although in Namibia and the western Cape some of these people latterly herded sheep and cattle. They were called the Bushmen by early European settlers but are now usually known as the San. Most of those in the southern part of the overall area succumbed to the expansion of farming over a century ago but to the north, in the Kalahari Desert, some continued to rely on hunting and gathering until recent times.

Because the paintings are usually in relatively exposed locations, in rock shelters or on rock outcrops, and because the pigments mainly consisted of iron oxides and charcoal mixed with melted animal fat or blood, it seems likely that many of the surviving paintings date only to the last few thousand years at most, older ones having weathered away. Certainly some of them were only done in recent centuries, as they depict men in European dress riding horses and carrying guns, and show cattle and cattle raids and in one case even a sailing ship. Nevertheless, seven slabs with naturalistic paintings of animals were found in deposits at Apollo 11 Cave, in southern Namibia, that have been dated to as much as 26,000 years ago. Painted stones and pieces of rock that had split off from painted surfaces and become buried in adjacent deposits have also been found in other archaeological sites and have been dated to various times over the last 7000 years. Dates obtained in this way are only minimum dates, of course, because the paintings might already have been old before the stone or rock fragment that they were on became buried. Direct dating of pigments might give more accurate dates but this still awaits systematic application. In the meantime, indications of the relative age of individual paintings can sometimes be obtained from the order in which they are painted on top of one another. Dating the rock engravings is also difficult but they appear to be contemporary with many of the paintings, engraved slabs from Wonderwerk Cave, in the interior of South Africa, having been found in deposits dating from 4000 to 10,000 years ago. Direct dating of the patina formed over other engravings has also indicated similar ages. Dating rock art is difficult but there are indications that the southern African art has a long history.

Most of the southern African paintings and engravings are quite small, some only a few centimetres long, yet they often show great attention to detail. Amongst the paintings the most common subjects are wild animals, human figures, domesticated animals, figures that are part human and part animal, handprints and animal paw-prints. Large numbers of representations are often grouped together and are frequently superimposed on one another. In some cases these groupings present narrative scenes, of people dancing, hunting or fighting. A range of colours was used, varying from purple through every tone of red and brown to yellow and including blacks and whites. Sometimes the paint seems to have been applied with fine brushes and considerable skill is evident, some representations consisting of several colours. Amongst the engravings human figures and groupings are less common but there are numerous geometric designs and otherwise many of the same subjects are present. There are three types of engravings: those consisting of fine, incised lines, that appear to be the oldest; animal representations made by hammering away the surface of the rock, that might be later in date; and geometric designs, that were thought to be the most recent but of which some might be much older. Nevertheless, in spite of variations in subject matter and technique, most of the rock art of southern Africa appears to have been the work of Khoisan-speaking later hunter-gatherers, as already stated. Any attempt to interpret it requires an understanding of their society.

Until less than 200 years ago parts of southern Africa were still occupied by the San people, some groups of whom continued to live in the Kalahari Desert until modern times. However, the desert environment offers few places suitable for painting or engraving and the desert-dwellers appear not to have practised rock art. It was their southern relatives who produced the art and continued to do so until gradually dispossessed, and often killed, by European settlers between 200 and 100 years ago. Thus painting and engraving had ceased by the time that Europeans took an interest in it but a small number of surviving southern San were able to inform scholars about their language, their way of life, and their rituals, myths and beliefs. To this information, recorded over a century ago, can be added extensive observations of the Kalahari San carried out much more recently. From these two sources it is apparent that the society to which the artists belonged was one of small groups, each of rarely more than 25 people. A group had no chief and its members could come and go at will but groups seem to have exploited particular areas, moving seasonally or at other times to make the best use of food and water resources. The men hunted a variety of animals, using the bow and arrow as well as trapping. Their arrows were so light that they would have had little effect, except that the heads were treated with poison and the arrows were so made that their shafts fell away on impact, leaving the poisoned point in the wound. Hunting and meat consumption were important but over half of what was eaten seems to have consisted of plant food collected by the women, including edible roots obtained by the use of digging sticks, each weighted with a bored stone.

As in all societies, there were tensions, arising in this case from personal disagreements, from sickness, and from uncertain availability of food. Dealing with such problems was the task of specially gifted men (and some women) who were able to communicate with the spirit world, people called 'shamans' by anthropologists. Some were recognized particularly as curers, some had power over the game, some could control the rain. To acquire the power to achieve these things, shamans would dance themselves into a trance, while women clapped and sang. Such trance dances brought on an altered state of consciousness, just as some drugs do, and it was believed that the shaman had literally entered the spirit world. In the process of entering a trance, he or she could tremble, sweat, bleed from the nose, and even collapse on the ground. Those who had gone through this experience described their sensations as feeling like flying or being under water. Furthermore, it appears that some of the shamans were actually the artists who produced the rock art and that in some cases they were depicting the hallucinations that they had experienced whilst in a trance. The rock art also included many depictions of the eland, the largest of the antelopes and one that was relatively easy to kill. However, to the San it was also important for reasons other than food. It played a major role in their myths and beliefs and was thought to be a source of power that could be exploited in the trance dance. It also figured in several other rituals. So great a part did the eland play in their lives, that some of the San considered themselves to be 'the people of the eland'.

The rock art reflects the life, rituals and beliefs of the San. For example, amongst the narrative scenes there are paintings of people in a characteristic bent-forward position, with blood pouring from the nose, clearly portraying

Figure 13 Red and white painting of a trance dance, those already in trance bleeding from the nose. Drakensberg, South Africa. Reproduced by permission of David Lewis-Williams from Lewis-Williams, J.D. 1983. *The rock art of southern Africa*. Cambridge University Press, Cambridge, part of Figure 7.

Figure 14 Painting of a hunter and an eland, overall length of eland 30 centimetres. Drakensberg, South Africa. Reproduced by permission of the Natal Museum from Vinnicombe, P. 1976. *People of the eland: rock paintings of the Drakensberg Bushmen as a reflection of their life and thought.* University of Natal Press, Pietermaritzburg, Figure 92.

the trance dance. Other paintings are representations of fantastic creatures, part human and part animal, that probably relate to the trance experience. Furthermore, paintings of eland outnumber those of other antelope and other animals, and the eland are painted in several colours and with considerable care, so that the paintings are often of great beauty. In addition, the eland are often shown dying, providing, it is thought, a metaphor for the shaman's trance. The engravings include subjects similar to those in the paintings and modern studies of the whole body of art have concluded that the San were using it to express beliefs of fundamental importance to them. As such, the art seems to have functioned as a communication system, in which metaphors and symbols gave it far more meaning than its representations would immediately suggest. In short, many of these were not merely pictures of animals and people but were a record of the most deeply felt ideas of the society that produced them. Indeed, they were probably more than that; in some cases they were sources of power that helped the shaman to enter the spirit world.

It is obviously difficult to recapture the thoughts of people long dead but this does appear to have been accomplished to some extent in the case of southern African rock art. Indeed, following this example, scholars conducting rock-art research in other parts of the world have also sought to explain representations in terms of shamans and altered states of consciousness. However, even in the case of southern African art, doubts have been expressed about current interpretations. For instance, to what extent can San beliefs and rituals, recorded during the last 100 years or so, be applied to art that is in some instances several thousands of years old? In response, it has been pointed out that there is marked continuity in subject matter over a very long period and that this would make it likely that similar ideas were represented. Whatever the truth of the matter, the southern African art does demonstrate how a people without literacy could still record their deepest emotions and do so in a manner that could be read by other members of their society.

6

PICTURES FROM A LOST WORLD

The rock art of the Sahara

The Sahara Desert has long been one of the most desolate parts of the world but many places within it have abundant archaeological evidence that this was not always so. Between about 11,000 and 4500 years ago, cooler and moister conditions than at present enabled groups of people to live in areas that now have few if any inhabitants (Chapter 7). Both their living sites and their burials are testimony to their presence and, most importantly, they left us pictures of the world in which they lived and of their part in it. These consist of both engravings and paintings that have been found on most of the substantial exposures of rock in the desert and which number in the tens of thousands. Most of them depict animals but people are also represented, as well as scenes from everyday life. Like the southern African rock art (Chapter 5), they are difficult to date but, unlike that art, they were prob-ably mainly the work of early food-producers such as herdsmen, rather than of hunter-gatherers. Also unlike the southern examples, the practice of art in the Saharan region virtually faded away after 2000 years ago, making its interpretation even more difficult. Nevertheless, the rock art of the Sahara has been extensively studied for many years by a large number of scholars. In spite of the problems that make it difficult to understand, the art yields information about life in the region before environmental change brought about abandonment by most of its occupants.

The Sahara is huge. Stretching over 4800 kilometres from the Atlantic to the Nile and bigger than the United States of America, it has been called the largest desert in the world. However, there is not merely one Sahara but many Saharas, that is to say the desert includes a wide range of environments for which the common factor is the absence or near absence of water. There are vast sand dunes, extensive sandy or rocky plains, great expanses of loose pebbles, and whole ranges of mountains. Inevitably it is in the latter that most of the rock art is found. Two of the most important areas are the Fezzan, in southern Libya, and Tassili-n-Ajjer, in southern Algeria, but also of significance are the Saharan Atlas, in northern Algeria, the Hoggar, in southern Algeria, and Tibesti, in northern Chad. Other areas include the Spanish Sahara, adjacent to the Atlantic coast, Ennedi, on the border between Chad and the Sudan, and Jebel Uweinat, at the junction of the borders of Libya, Egypt and the Sudan. Rock art also occurs elsewhere and this widespread distribution makes it difficult to generalize about the art as a whole. For instance, attempts to identify changes in the subject and style of the art as time passed will almost certainly be complicated by regional variations between bodies of art, which in some cases are very long distances from one another. Developments that took place in one region at a particular time might have occurred earlier or later in another.

Nevertheless, for many years Saharan rock art was arranged in a neat sequence that was applied to the whole desert. Absolute dates were rare, so the relative order of different examples of the art was obtained by grouping thousands of images into classes, based on similar patina, characteristic animals or objects depicted, technique, and style. Superimposition of artwork, the changing environment and fauna of the desert, the date and subsistence economy of occupation sites associated with rock art, and a knowledge of the Sahara's later history, were then used to create an overall timetable. This consisted of four phases, named after their most characteristic subjects. First, was the Bubaline Phase, from about 8000 to about 5000 years ago, during which many engravings were made of an extinct buffalo, *Bubalus antiquus*. Contemporary with this was the Round Head Phase, characterized by paintings of human figures with round featureless heads. Second was the Bovidian Phase, from about 5000 to about 3000 years ago, during which paintings and engravings of herds of cattle were common. Third was the Horse Phase, from about 3000 to about 2000 years ago, in which horses were frequently depicted in both paintings and engravings. Fourth and last was the Camel Phase, from about 2000 years ago until the present, during which camels were often represented in paintings and engravings. Ongoing research has now modified this overall sequence in a number of respects, particularly to allow for regional variations, and most of the dates have been revised.

Rock art of the Bubaline Phase consists of large naturalistic engravings of animals, including *Bubalus antiquus*, rhinoceros, elephants, hippopotami, giraffes, ostriches, lions, antelope, and cattle and sheep (both formerly presumed wild). The engravings are deeply cut and often polished. There are no rock paintings. Human figures also occur, some with animal heads, carrying clubs, sticks, axes and bows. It was long thought that the animals depicted during this phase were all wild and that therefore the art belonged to a time before the domestication of animals. However, it has now been shown that domesticated cattle, sheep, goats and donkeys do occur during the Bubaline Phase. For this reason it is has been suggested that the phase began only about 6000 years ago. Furthermore, it seems that it probably came to an end at different times in different regions, because the wild animals represented, most of which have long vanished from the Sahara, are unlikely to have died out simultaneously in every part of the desert. Thus the Bubaline Phase is

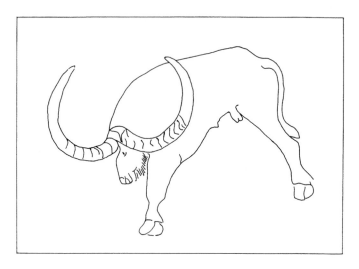

Figure 15 Engraving of *Bubalus antiquus*, Algeria. After McBurney, C.B.M. 1960. *The Stone Age of Northern Africa*. Penguin, Harmondsworth, Plate 7.

Figure 16 Engraving of milking scene, Wadi Tiksatin, Libya. Reproduced by permission of Michael Rainsbury from Rainsbury, M. 2003. Prehistoric Society Tour to South West Libya 14–21 October 2002. *Past: the Newsletter of the Prehistoric Society* 43, Figure 3.

thought to have lingered on in the Saharan Atlas and the Fezzan until about 3000 years ago, in contrast to Tassili-n-Ajjer, where it concluded at the beginning of an arid period about 4500 years ago. As for the paintings of the Round Head Phase, these do appear to be roughly contemporary with the Bubaline engravings and in Tassili-n-Ajjer they might continue until about 3000 years ago. Such paintings also occur in the Fezzan and in Ennedi, and are characterized by human figures ranging in size from small to gigantic and often painted in a number of colours. It is uncertain whether the blank faces were deliberate or merely result from weathering of the painted surface but some figures appear to be wearing masks and it has been suggested that this art had a ritual significance. In addition to the human figures, there are also representations of the same animals as in the Bubaline Phase, although without *Bubalus antiquus* itself. Thus it appears that the Bubaline Phase and the Round Head Phase represent different art styles rather than different periods.

The Bovidian Phase is characterized by paintings of herds of cattle, often shown with their herdsmen. They are usually painted in a number of colours and there are also engravings, although they are smaller and less deeply cut than formerly. Many of the paintings are remarkably informative about the life of those who produced them. Particularly in Tassili-n-Ajjer, there are scenes of conflict, hunting, travelling, camping, dancing, herding and milking. In addition, depictions of huts, beds, pots, clothing, body ornaments, bows, throwing sticks, shields and spears can be found amongst the art. The cattle are shown in great detail, including their markings, their udders and the varying shape of their horns. Sheep, goats and dogs are also shown. The existence of herds of domesticated cattle, in parts of the Sahara where no cattle can survive today, is a powerful indicator of the environmental changes that have subsequently taken place. The Bovidian Phase is thought to have commenced about 6000 years ago and in Tassili-n-Ajjer was contemporary with the Bubaline Phase until the onset of the arid period about 4500 years ago. However, with the return of somewhat moister conditions after about 3500 years ago, there was a resumption of the Bovidian art. It seems that not only is the Bovidian Phase a style rather than a period but that even as a style it is a somewhat artificial grouping of art that occurs widely in the Sahara over a considerable length of time. Nevertheless, it provides important evidence for early domesticated cattle in the desert (Chapter 7).

Thus the first two phases of the conventional sequence of Saharan rock art are now thought to overlap each other. However, the third and fourth phases of the old sequence have survived without much alteration, mainly because they are identified in each case by the appearance of an animal known to have been introduced into the Sahara, even if the date for this remains somewhat uncertain. The first of these is the Horse Phase, the dating of which might be slightly revised to between about 2700 and about 2000 years ago. Consisting of both paintings and engravings, this phase has been divided into two, its first half being characterized by horses pulling wheeled vehicles, and its second by human figures mounted on horses. Many of the depictions of vehicles show two-wheeled chariots, pulled by two galloping horses and containing a single charioteer, but there is considerable variation and much of the artwork is very schematic. Some of the chariots are shown without horses, some vehicles have four not two wheels and were presumably carts not chariots, and some vehicles are shown drawn by oxen not by horses. Historical accounts in the lands fringing the eastern Mediterranean record the earlier importance of horse-drawn chariots in warfare and their subsequent popularity for racing. It might have been the latter activity that caught the Saharan rock artist's attention but there has been much discussion of the distribution of the various representations of wheeled vehicles. They have been found along two rough lines ending south of the desert at the great bend of the Niger River and originating respectively in Libya and Morocco. These 'chariot tracks', as they have been called, have been claimed as evidence for trade across the Sahara some 2500 years ago but the argument has been much criticized and there is no other archaeological evidence to support it (Chapter 18). In the second half of the Horse Phase depictions of chariots were largely superseded by mounted armed men, often shown in a schematic fashion. Towards the end of this horseman period, even writing appeared amongst the rock art, in the form of Libyco-Berber script. Otherwise, the overall Horse Phase continued to include representations of cattle and of wild animals, although the larger species of the latter were no longer shown.

The fourth and final part of the Saharan rock art sequence is the Camel Phase, commencing about 2000 years ago and continuing until the present time. During the early part of this phase both horses and camels were depicted but as conditions in the desert became progressively drier the horse was no longer included. However, human figures continued to be represented, as well as some wild animals and cattle and goats, but in an increasingly schematic fashion. Artistically, the artwork shows degeneration and eventually became mere graffiti. Consisting of both paintings and engravings, it was commonly accompanied by Tifinagh script or by Arabic script and some geometric designs also appeared. Clearly, Saharan rock art gradually died as the environments that had supported its artists deteriorated to their present condition.

Because the greater part of the Saharan rock art was done so long ago, it is particularly difficult to interpret it objectively and to decide its purpose. Probably it was done for a number of reasons; sometimes, for example, to illustrate oral traditions, at other times as a part of important rituals. However, one thing is certain. In spite of the dating difficulties, changes in the art reflect the later history of the Saharan environment and of human adaptations to it. A world that included water-loving hippopotami and herds of cattle was gradually replaced by one which only the drought-resistant camel could tolerate. The real value of Saharan rock art is that it provides us with pictures from a lost world.

7

PRODUCING FOOD

Early developments in North and West Africa

At one time all the human beings in the world were hunters, gatherers and fishers, essentially they were collectors of food not producers. Indeed, some groups of people continued to live in this way until recent times and in many places lived quite well. Nevertheless, during the last 10,000 years or so major changes took place, in which most humans came to control their sources of food, so that they could produce it at will. This involved manipulating the reproduction of selected animals and plants, so that they were more suited to human requirements. The result was the development of farming, the most important change in subsistence economy that has ever taken place. It consisted of two major elements: pastoralism, the herding of domesticated animals, and cultivation, the growing of domesticated plants. Sometimes these activities characterized different groups of people, sometimes they were practised to varying degrees by the same people. The changes that led to farming used to be thought of as an economic 'revolution'. It was also thought that these changes had originated in a limited number of places and had then diffused to many other parts of the world. In the case of Africa, its proximity to South-West Asia, where there was very early evidence for farming, seemed to be sufficient proof of introduction from that region. However, archaeologists have now realized that the shift from food collection to food production in Africa was a very gradual process, involving many different developments in many places. Some of these developments did indeed originate in South-West Asia but it is becoming increasingly apparent that African innovation was also a major factor.

The change from collecting to producing food took a long time because domesticating animals and plants was a slow process of genetic modification. Animals had to be bred that were more docile, plants had to be grown whose edible parts were larger or more easily exploited. Clearly, the beginning of this process of change is difficult to identify, simply because the animals and plants concerned would still have been so like their wild relatives. Thus there is no point at which it can be said that farming was 'invented', rather it was the culmination of a series of changes so gradual that even the people involved may not have been conscious of them. Indeed, the origins of those changes are to be found in the intensification of hunter-gatherer economies discussed in Chapter 4. Why the change to food production should have occurred has long been a subject of debate but complex responses to environmental fluctuations are likely to have been factors of importance. For instance, some of the earliest developments took place in what is now the Sahara Desert, where a long dry period ended about 11,000 years ago, giving way to the cooler, moister conditions of what is sometimes called (with exaggeration) 'the green Sahara'. Although those conditions persisted until about 4500 years ago, they were frequently interrupted by drier periods of varying lengths. These changes in Saharan environments alternately tempted and punished its human inhabitants. When conditions were good, stone-using hunter-gatherers were able to expand into regions where they then became vulnerable to any subsequent deterioration in the environment, requiring a variety of adaptive strategies to survive (Chapter 4). Amongst these were the hunting of wild cattle and the collection of wild grass seeds. Not surprisingly, it was in parts of the Sahara that some of these wild cattle and wild grass seeds were eventually domesticated.

The first indication of such a change is at the eastern Saharan site of Nabta Playa, in the far south of Egypt. By about 9000 years ago stone-using people at this place were keeping domesticated cattle and using pottery, although they were still hunting and collecting wild grasses and fruits. Pits and traces of huts indicate some stability of settlement, even if only seasonal. It has been argued that the cattle must have been domesticated because the contemporary environment was so marginal that they could not have existed without human care. Inevitably this has been disputed but there is also evidence for domesticated cattle at Enneri Bardagué, in northern Chad, before 7000 years ago, and at Uan Muhuggiag, in western Libya, Grotte Capeletti, in northern Algeria, and Adrar Bous, in northern Niger, before 6000 years ago. Collectively these early dates make it unlikely that domesticated cattle were introduced into Africa from elsewhere, and the probability that the Sahara was one of several places in the world where cattle were first domesticated is also supported by mitochondrial DNA evidence. Significantly, the earliest dates for domesticated cattle become progressively later further to the west and south, in the margins of the desert and in the savanna. As conditions deteriorated in the Sahara, groups of cattle pastoralists moved particularly to the south, into areas that in previous moister periods had been infested by tsetse flies and therefore unhealthy for both cattle and people.

In contrast to the situation with cattle, there were no wild sheep or goats in the Sahara from which the domesticated varieties could have been derived and it is therefore thought that they were both introduced from South-West Asia. They were present at Nabta Playa and Grotte Capeletti by about 7000 years ago and were probably adopted rapidly in the Sahara because of their tolerance of dry conditions. Far to the south-west, the inhabitants of extensive partly stone-built settlements at Dhar Tichitt, in Mauritania, were

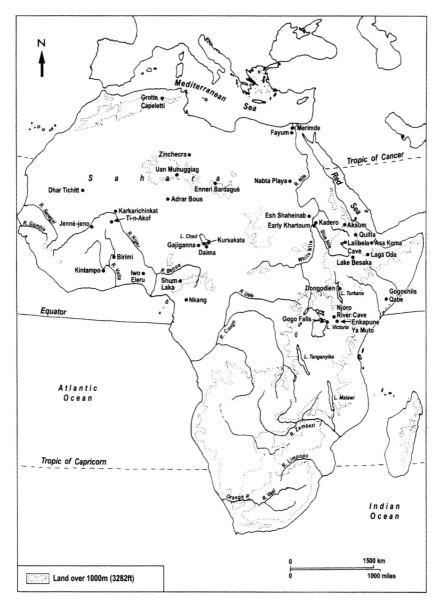

Figure 17 Early food-production sites in the northern half of Africa. Refer to Chapters 7 and 8. Map by Sue Singleton.

Figure 18 Modern pearl millet. This was the first domesticated cereal for which there is evidence in the western Sahara and in the West African savanna.

keeping both cattle and goats by about 3500 years ago. In addition, they were growing indigenous pearl millet, which had already been domesticated somewhere in the Sahara or on its edges and appears to have been the first African domesticated cereal. Indeed, Dhar Tichitt provides the earliest certain evidence for crop cultivation in this part of Africa and it is thus apparent that pastoralism developed before cultivation in the Saharan area. Nevertheless, by about 2500 years ago cultivation was well established, as is evident at Zinchecra, in Libya, where emmer-wheat, barley, date, grape and fig were being grown at that time.

Wheat and barley must have been diffused from the lower Nile Valley of Egypt, to which they had been introduced from South-West Asia by about 7000 years ago. Domesticated animals had also been introduced from the same region and the adoption of pastoralism and cultivation in Egypt seems to have been relatively sudden and at about the same time. At Merimde, on the western side of the Nile delta, for instance, stone-using village-dwellers who had pottery were cultivating barley, emmer-wheat and flax, and keeping cattle, sheep, goats, pigs and dogs, from about 7000 years ago. At about the same time settlements in the Fayum Depression, west of the lower Nile, had a similar economy. It was from this general base in and around the Nile Valley that the Predynastic cultures developed, consisting of a succession of stone-using farming societies who gradually adopted the use of copper and from which emerged the earliest dynasties of Ancient Egypt by about 5000 years ago.

Far up the Nile, in the Sudan, the stone-using people of Esh Shaheinab had domesticated goats and cattle about 6000 years ago but fishing was still important and they had pottery similar to that of their hunter-gatherer predecessors at the site of Early Khartoum, in the same region. At a similar date to Esh Shaheinab, cattle, sheep and goats were herded at Kadero, also in the Sudan. In addition, wild sorghum, finger millet and panicum were exploited and might have been cultivated, hunting and fishing being marginal activities. By about 5000 years ago there were other farmers along the middle Nile, cultivating wheat and barley and herding sheep, goats and cattle but it is remarkable that the earliest evidence for cultivated sorghum is only about 2000 years old. This indigenous African cereal must have been domesticated much earlier, because it was already being cultivated in Saudi Arabia and India, where it was not indigenous, some 4500 years ago.

In the West African savanna, as in the Sahara, pastoralism appeared before cultivation, although somewhat later than in the desert. Cattle-herders who also kept sheep or goats were present at Karkarichinkat, in Mali, by about 4000 years ago, at Gajiganna, near Lake Chad, by about 3000 years ago, and at Daima, in the same part of Nigeria, by a little later (on Gajiganna and Daima see Chapter 14). The earliest evidence for cultivation was again domesticated pearl millet: at Birimi, in northern Ghana, a little over 3000 years ago, at Ti-n-Akof, in Burkina Faso, about 3000 years ago, and at Kursakata, in north-east Nigeria (Chapter 14), by about 2500 years ago. The important crops in the savanna were all cereals that were indigenous to Africa and consisted of pearl millet, West African rice and sorghum. However, as in the middle Nile, the earliest known cultivated sorghum is only about 2000 years old and comes from the site of Jenné-jeno, in Mali (Chapter 17). The earliest evidence for domesticated West African rice comes from the same site and is of a similar date.

In the West African rainforest and its margins things were different. Conditions were not suitable for the cultivation of cereals. Tsetse fly, that spread trypanosomiasis amongst domesticated livestock and sleeping sickness amongst people, discouraged the development of pastoralism. Although some cattle and goats have been kept in the forest long enough to have developed resistance to trypanosomiasis, plant food has long been more important. In particular, two African species of yam and the indigenous oil-palm seem to have played a leading role. Evidence for early farming is limited but one of the sites at Kintampo, in Ghana, produced oil-palm nuts and possibly cultivated cowpeas from a context dated to over 3000 years ago, as well as indications that cattle and sheep were kept by people who also hunted and gathered. In addition, evidence from Iwo Eleru, in Nigeria, might suggest moves towards food production. At that site, pottery and ground stone axes first appeared over 5000 years ago and after about 4500 years ago some of the microliths had sheen on their edges, as if used for cutting plant material, and grindstones became more common. Further east, at Shum Laka, in Cameroon, pottery was in use before 4000 years ago, along with partly polished flaked stone artefacts that resemble hoes. However, some of the most useful evidence comes from the Cameroon site of Nkang, which has produced evidence for banana growing over 2000 years ago, as well as evidence for domesticated sheep and goats and for hunting, gathering and fishing. Bananas are not indigenous to Africa and must have been introduced from South-East Asia via the East African coast. That they had reached the West African rainforest by such an early date would suggest that cultivation and management of local plants and trees was already well established, as perhaps was also the case in the equatorial rainforest to the south.

There are still large gaps in our understanding of early food production in Africa but for the northern and western parts of the continent a basic framework is emerging. It seems that pastoralism developed first, probably as an outcome of hunter-gatherer strategies to cope with environmental fluctuation in the Sahara. These led to the domestication of wild cattle that were present in the desert and ultimately to the domestication of some of the wild grasses, of which pearl millet seems to have been the first. Sheep and goats were also adopted, after their introduction from South-West Asia to the Nile Valley, in the latter area being accompanied by wheat and barley. Subsequently, both pastoralism and cultivation spread from the Sahara into the West African savanna and from the lower Nile to the middle reaches of the river. However, in the West African rainforest different food production strategies had to be developed, based on yams and oil-palms with relatively little input from domesticated animals. Finally, it should be noted that in all cases Africa's earliest farmers still had only stone tools, quite remarkable for people who contributed to the most important change in human subsistence that has ever taken place.

8

PRODUCING FOOD

Adaptation in North-East and East Africa

From the previous chapter it is apparent that early farmers produced food in a variety of ways, using different plants and animals. This was particularly the case in North-East and East Africa, where introduced species were exploited along with others that were specific to parts of the region and in some cases unknown elsewhere. Consequently, there was a wide range of adaptations across a large section of the continent, comprising the modern countries of Ethiopia, Eritrea, Djibouti, Somalia, Kenya and Uganda, along with parts of the Sudan and Tanzania. The situation was further complicated by the persistence in more southerly areas of hunter-gatherers and the often heavy reliance of early farmers on a continuation of hunting. In addition, the amount of archaeological research that has been carried out into the development of food-production in these areas varies greatly. This makes it difficult to get a general picture of what was happening and sometimes leads to doubt about the interpretation of the evidence that is available. Nevertheless, it appears that domesticated animals and plants spread into the region from the north and west before 6000 years ago, consisting mainly of cattle, sheep and goats, and wheat and barley. The latter cereals were supplemented on the Ethiopian Plateau by teff, a locally domesticated cereal, and further south replaced by finger millet and sorghum because of the different environment. However, pastoralism appears to have become the prevailing economy in much of southern East Africa, although its extent was limited by the tsetse fly, which initially prevented its spread south of northern Tanzania.

The detailed picture must have been much more complex. The principal reason for this is the great diversity of environments in this region of Africa, particularly because of its wide range of altitudes, from below sea-level to above 2000 metres. This results in a variety of rainfall patterns, from desert in parts of Eritrea, to semi-desert in northern Kenya, to places with heavy rainfall in Ethiopia and Uganda. Different temperature regimes at different heights further complicate the situation, as do varying seasonal patterns and soil character. All these factors must have influenced decisions about what could be grown and when it could be grown, as well as which livestock

Figure 19 Painting of long-horned, humpless cattle and herdsmen, Dire Dawa, Ethiopia. Reproduced by permission of the publishers from Clark, J.D. 1970. *The prehistory of Africa*. Thames and Hudson, London, Figure 67.

could be grazed in which area and at what time of the year. Add to this the presence of climatic fluctuations over time and of complex interactions between farming and hunter-gathering, and the result is a kaleidoscope of subsistence economies, of which the available archaeological evidence provides only brief and scattered glimpses.

Some of the most evocative but frustrating evidence consists of rock paintings in Eritrea, Ethiopia and Somalia, that depict herds of apparently domesticated cattle. The problem is that these are not easy to interpret and they are very difficult to date. Nevertheless, paintings showing long-horned humpless cattle but lacking depictions of humped cattle or camels, that were only introduced to the region during the last 2000 years or so, are presumed to record early pastoral activities. Some indication of the time to which these might belong has been provided by animal bones from Asa Koma, in Djibouti, which indicate the presence of domesticated cattle by about 3500 years ago. Similar evidence from Laga Oda and Lake Besaka, in Ethiopia, show that cattle were also there at the same date, at the latter site with sheep or goats. Furthermore, cattle and sheep or goats were present at Gogoshiis Qabe, in Somalia, by a date earlier than 3500 years ago. Indeed, indications that domesticated cattle were on the Ethiopian Plateau by about 5000 years ago have been provided by the reanalysis of an old excavation at Quiha, in northern Ethiopia, but the dating of the evidence is unsatisfactory. On the basis of the distribution of their wild ancestors, it is also possible that cats, donkeys and guinea-fowl were domesticated somewhere in the eastern part of Africa. In addition, there were later introductions, probably as a result of trading contacts, that included the humped cattle and camels already mentioned but also fat-tailed sheep, chickens and horses.

Concerning the early cultivation of plants, archaeology provides even less information. Thus there is evidence of domesticated barley, horse beans and chickpeas, as well as of cattle and sheep or goats, from Lalibela Cave, in Ethiopia, but only at a date of a little over 2000 years ago. Similarly, sites at Aksum, in northern Ethiopia (Chapter 12), have produced evidence of barley, teff, various wheats, finger millet, sorghum, various pulses, oil and fibre plants (including flax and cotton), fruits and vegetables, but only from periods between about 1500 and 2500 years ago. This lack of earlier evidence is remarkable for an area which, particularly in the case of Ethiopia, has such a wide range of cultivated plants. Quite probably the situation is the result of limited archaeological research, because both botanical and linguistic evidence suggest a high antiquity for food production in Ethiopia. For instance, the introduced cereals wheat and barley have been grown there long enough for a large number of varieties to develop, some of them exclusive to the region. In addition, there are a number of Ethiopian domesticated plants, such as the cereal teff, the oil-plant noog, ensete (a banana-like plant of which the stem and root are eaten), and the stimulants coffee and chat. These are indigenous to the region and were presumably domesticated there, a process that probably took a considerable time. Furthermore, the ox-drawn

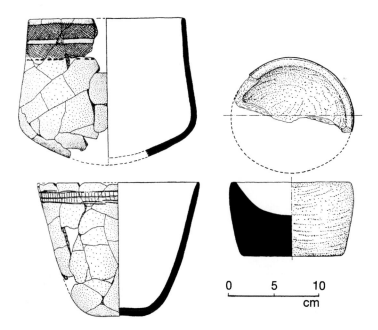

Figure 20 Two pots and a stone bowl (to right) from Narosura, Kenya. Reproduced by permission of the British Institute in Eastern Africa from Odner, K. 1972. Excavations at Narosura, a stone bowl site in the Southern Kenyan Highlands. *Azania* 7, parts of Figures 18 and 21.

plough was already in use in Ethiopia before 2000 years ago, this being its furthest south in Africa until modern times. It seems quite likely that it was adopted at an early date, along with wheat and barley cultivation. Significantly, linguistic evidence suggests that the herding of domesticated animals and the cultivation of cereals may have started in Ethiopia as early as 6000 to 7000 years ago.

Archaeological evidence from further south, in northern Kenya, also suggests an early date for farming in North-East Africa, from where it was probably introduced to East Africa. For instance, domesticated sheep or goats and cattle were present at the site of Dongodien, close to the eastern shore of Lake Turkana, by about 4000 years ago. The people at this place were using pottery and stone tools. Fishing remained important and hunting was still practised. Even further south, in southern Kenya, the site of Enkapune Ya Muto has evidence of domesticated goats by about 3000 years ago and perhaps earlier. At other sites in central, southern and western Kenya and in northern Tanzania, there is also evidence for the herding of cattle and the keeping of sheep and goats by about 2500 years ago. Many of the living sites of the people involved are near the limits of archaeological visibility, having been occupied by mobile pastoralists who had little or no interest in cultivation. Indeed, at one time they were better known from their burial sites. Nevertheless, it is apparent that they had stone tools that were often made from obsidian, a volcanic glass that is excellent flaking material and has razor-sharp edges. They also possessed pottery and distinctive stone bowls and pestles that were probably used for the preparation of plant food. There appear to have been many of these pastoral groups, the relationships of which are difficult to establish. One of them, situated on the western side of the Kenyan Rift Valley, is called by archaeologists the Elmenteitan. Its people are perhaps best known from their remarkable site at Njoro River Cave, that had evidence from a little over 3000 years ago indicating the unusual practice for Africa of cremating the dead. Other groups, who also used stone tools, pottery and stone bowls, buried their dead under stone cairns or in crevices between rocks but without cremation. Collectively, the archaeological evidence tends to agree with the linguistic evidence, that suggests movements of pastoralists into Kenya from further north.

When they got there, they probably interacted with hunter-gatherers already in the region and might have obtained plant food from them. Indeed, it seems likely that the early pastoralists were often partly dependent on hunting and gathering themselves. The degree to which this was the case probably varied from group to group and from time to time, depending on the environment exploited and on seasonal conditions. However, the rarity of evidence for plant food in relevant sites makes it difficult to know just how much pastoralists did make use of plants in their diet. In particular, this raises questions about the extent to which they practised cultivation as well as pastoralism. Before the introduction of the Central American crop maize in recent centuries, it seems that finger millet and sorghum were the staples in much of East Africa, and it is very likely that this had also been the case for several thousand years previously. Sorghum is generally thought to have been domesticated further north, in the eastern Sahara or adjacent savanna, but both genetic and linguistic evidence suggest that finger millet was probably domesticated in northern Uganda. If this was the case, then it must have been cultivated in East Africa for a long time.

Thus the early food-producers of East Africa could have practised a broad spectrum of subsistence strategies, in which pastoralism was combined with hunter-gathering or cultivation or both, the relative proportions of each varying greatly. This might partly explain the survival until recent times of groups of East African hunter-gatherers, who could exploit such abundant wild animal resources. It would also suggest that highly specialized cattle pastoralists in East Africa, such as the Maasai of Kenya or the Barabaig of Tanzania, were a somewhat later development. This might have been an adaptation to possibly drier conditions during the last 2000 years or so, facilitated by the introduction of drought-resistant humped cattle, ultimately from South Asia. Indeed, even semi-desert was ultimately exploited by pastoralists, when some of them, such as the Rendille of northern Kenya, took to herding and milking camels instead of cattle. However, drier conditions could also have opened up areas to pastoralists from which they had been previously excluded by tsetse fly. This seems to have been particularly the case to the south, where the southern limit of pastoralism appears for some time to have been northern Tanzania. It was probably only about 2000 years ago that climatic changes opened up fly-free corridors that allowed pastoralism to expand further to the south, domesticated sheep reaching the southern tip of the continent soon afterwards. Also by that time, many people in East and Central Africa had iron tools and cultivation was becoming well established, in the process clearing woodland and helping to reduce the extent of the tsetse-infested areas.

Little is known of early farming in far western Kenya and Uganda, although it is possible that the makers of what is known as Kansyore pottery were cattle pastoralists. Evidence for this was dated to over 3000 years ago at the site of Gogo Falls, near the Kenyan side of Lake Victoria, but has been treated with caution. Nevertheless, the subsequent importance of agriculture around the lake and between it and the lakes of the Western Rift Valley suggests that the origins of farming must have been early. In particular, cattle herding and banana cultivation could have had a long history in the area, cattle having reached northern Kenya about 4000 years ago, and bananas, introduced to East Africa from South-East Asia, having crossed the continent to Cameroon by over 2000 years ago.

The earliest farming in North-East and East Africa consisted of a great number of differing adaptations to a complex range of environments. Introduced crops were supplemented or replaced by a variety of locally domesticated plants. The herding of introduced animals was combined to varying extents with hunter-gathering or cultivation or both. Given the often patchy archaeological evidence that is available in many areas and the complete lack of evidence in some, it is difficult to reconstruct the overall changes in subsistence and culture that occurred. However, one thing is apparent: it is misleading to separate people into neat categories of hunter-gatherer, pastoralist, and cultivator. Early farming in this part of Africa is a powerful reminder that these subsistence economies are merely strategies on an adaptive continuum. Environmental conditions, in particular the amount of rainfall and its variation through space and time, could strongly influence the position of any group of people on that continuum and even result in a change in that position. In short, it was all about adaptation.

9

THE POWER OF METAL

The origins of African iron-working

Most people in Africa moved directly from making and using stone and bone tools to making and using iron ones. In the greater part of the continent there seems to have been no intermediate period when copper and bronze tools were made and used, as in Europe and Asia. Consequently, for a long time archaeologists assumed that a knowledge of iron-smelting and blacksmithing must have been introduced to Africa from the Mediterranean world, and probably at a late date. However, excavations have now shown that African iron-working is older than was thought and could have been the result of indigenous invention. The matter is still not resolved satisfactorily but it is clear that the introduction of iron did have long-term repercussions of great importance, providing more efficient tools, as well as more effective weapons. Yet in the short term its adoption seems often to have been slow, depending on its availability and the extent of cultural conservatism, so that its impact was probably variable. Nevertheless, iron technology eventually changed the face of much of the continent, commencing in West and Central Africa over 2500 years ago and reaching parts of southern Africa by about 1500 years ago.

Smelting iron by the method employed in precolonial Africa is not an easy process. Iron melts at the very high temperature of 1540°C but the resulting product is cast iron, that is too brittle to be worked by a blacksmith. In the Western world cast iron only became important a little over 500 years ago, when Europeans developed blast furnaces, although the Chinese had made and used it 2000 years earlier. In Africa and for a long time in the West it was wrought iron that was wanted, because it could be hammered and bent and drawn into many shapes. This was produced in a bloomery furnace, at temperatures of 1150 to 1200°C. A mixture of iron oxide ore and charcoal was heated in a furnace that was often quite small, using hand-operated bellows that forced air into the furnace through one or more clay pipes built into its side. It was essential not only to reach the desired temperature but to achieve a low level of carbon dioxide and a high level of carbon monoxide within the furnace. This reduced the iron oxide ore, leaving a 'bloom', a spongy mass of metallic iron and slag. Subsequently

51

Figure 21 Bloomery furnace being prepared for smelting iron, Toumra, western Sudan. Reproduced by permission of Gunnar Haaland from Haaland, G. and others 2002. The social life of iron. *Anthropos* 97, Figure 2.

this had to be repeatedly heated and hammered to remove the slag and produce wrought iron. The main problem with the bloomery process was that air had to be blown into the furnace to burn the fuel and reach the desired temperature but too much oxygen could stop the reduction, or reverse it and reoxidize the iron ore.

Both knowledge and experience must have been necessary for the earliest use of this process but apparently metallurgy was previously unknown in much of Africa. This being the case, for a long time archaeologists argued that a knowledge of iron technology must have been introduced from outside the continent. It seems that the earliest smelting of the metal was over 3000 years ago in what is now Turkey. From there, knowledge of iron-working appears to have spread to Western Europe by almost 3000 years ago and to have reached North Africa and Egypt a little later. From Egypt, the technology was apparently diffused up the Nile and was known at Meroë, in the Sudan, by about 2500 years ago. At this place there are huge mounds of iron slag, indicating the importance of the iron industry there, and it seemed an obvious conclusion that it must have been from there that the necessary technological knowledge reached the rest of Africa. However, this idea had to be abandoned about thirty years ago when a number of iron furnaces excavated at Taruga, in central Nigeria, were found to be at least

2500 years old. This made them at least as old as the earliest evidence for iron at Meroë and certainly older than the oldest furnaces that had been found there, which significantly were of a different design. As a result of this new information, archaeologists turned to another source from which a knowledge of iron-working could have been diffused. This was Carthage, on the north coast of Africa in what is now Tunisia, a city known to have been founded by the Phoenicians about 2800 years ago (Chapter 15). They were a people who were already making and using iron but there remained the question of how their skills had crossed the Sahara, at a time when communications through the desert seem at best to have been limited. In addition, there was no direct archaeological evidence for iron-smelting at Carthage, with which the known African evidence could be compared. Furthermore, as time went on, more and more excavated evidence from tropical Africa was found to be as old or older than the foundation of Carthage. Increasingly, diffusion looked doubtful.

Archaeological evidence for early iron-working in Africa is limited by the fact that objects made of the metal deteriorate rapidly in most tropical soils, in some cases leaving little more than a rusty stain. However, the remains of smelting furnaces and their bellows pipes are usually of clay that has been fired by use and they frequently survive well, even if fragmented. When excavated, furnaces often still contain a little charcoal, that can be dated using the radiocarbon technique, and some slag that can be informative about the process that was in use. Collections of iron ore are also sometimes found in the vicinity of excavated furnaces, and isolated finds of slag can indicate the presence of smelting even when no furnace remains can be located. In the case of Taruga in Nigeria, already mentioned, and of Do Dimi in Niger, and Otumbi in Gabon, furnace remains date back to more than 2500 years ago. Other evidence, which is as early or almost as early, has been found in Cameroon, the Central African Republic and Congo. Indeed, at several sites in Rwanda and Burundi evidence for iron-smelting has been dated to over 3000 years ago, although the reliability of some of these dates has been questioned. Overall, the evidence now shows that iron-smelting was already established in West and Central Africa before 2500 years ago, at dates that make an origin from outside the continent unlikely and which suggest that indigenous innovation might have been responsible.

It has been argued that excavated evidence for iron-smelting at Kemondo Bay, at the edge of Lake Victoria in north-west Tanzania, gives strong support to the possibility of such an independent African invention of iron-working. Claims have been made that, prior to 2000 years ago, iron-smelters at that place were employing a unique one-step process that produced steel from their furnaces rather then iron blooms. This 'direct steel process', as it has been called, produced cast iron as well as steel and required higher temperatures than those normally reached in a bloomery furnace. These were obtained, it was thought, by the use of longer bellows pipes set deep into

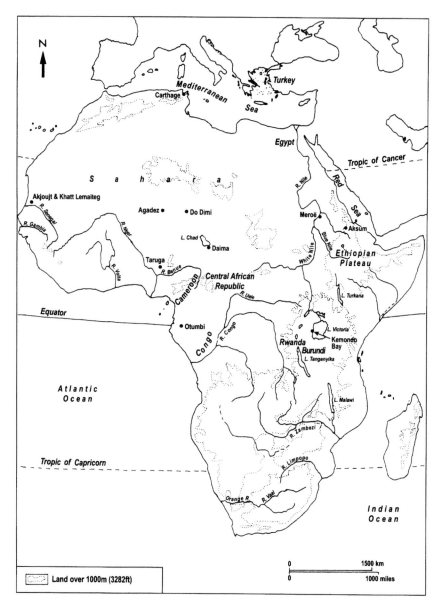

Figure 22 Sites and areas with evidence for early metallurgy. Refer to Chapter 9.
Map by Sue Singleton.

the furnace, so that the air from the bellows was preheated by the time that it reached the ore and charcoal within the furnace. It appeared that the existence of such a unique technique must mean that African iron-smelting was an indigenous development. However, the evidence has been criticized on technical grounds; apparently the direct steel process was not unique to Africa but was also known in Europe at a similar date. Moreover, it now seems that the temperature of the air blown into the furnace by the longer pipes would not have been raised significantly by preheating. Nevertheless, although the Kemondo Bay evidence does not prove that iron-smelting in Africa was an indigenous invention, it does provide another example of its early practice and indeed its practice at an apparently sophisticated level.

It is also necessary to re-examine the assumption that metallurgy was unknown in most of Africa prior to the introduction of iron. In Ancient Egypt copper was being produced and used more than 5000 years ago and bronze was adopted by about 3500 to 4000 years ago. However, although copper was in use by people along the middle Nile by about 3500 years ago and perhaps by a similar date on the Ethiopian Plateau, its earliest use in other parts of the continent does not seem to have predated that of iron. Evidence from furnaces, slag and artefacts show that copper was being smelted at Akjoujt in western Mauritania and Agadez in Niger by about 2500 to 3000 years ago, in other words at a date similar to that for the earliest African iron-smelting. At Khatt Lemaiteg, in Mauritania, and at Agadez, there have been claims of evidence at an earlier date but these are thought to be unreliable. Nevertheless, we might not have heard the last of early copper-smelting in tropical Africa, there could be crucial evidence that has still not been discovered.

It is also interesting to note that the copper ores in Mauritania contain a high iron content. It has been suggested that this would have helped the smelting of the copper but that in the process some droplets of iron or of iron slag could have been formed. The development of African iron-smelting might thus have been an accidental outcome of indigenous copper-smelting. Similarly, it has been pointed out that from about 6000 years ago crushed iron ore was used to coat the surface of some of the pottery made along the middle and lower Nile. Controlled firing then resulted in a pot of which part was fired red in an oxidizing environment and part was fired black in a reducing environment. In doing this, temperatures would have been reached not much below those necessary for the reduction of iron ore in a bloomery furnace. So here again is a way in which iron-smelting might have been accidentally discovered in Africa itself. It is also relevant to note that iron ore, of a variety of types, is widely available in many parts of the continent and there are a number of other circumstances in which its potential might have been realized. As yet we cannot be sure of the origins of African iron-working but the possibility of it being an indigenous development certainly needs close consideration.

Although the question of the origins of African iron-working has attracted much attention from researchers, there is also the problem of the nature and extent of its impact on African societies. It is surely the case that the possession of iron tools would have greatly improved people's capacity to modify their environment. It would have been easier to cultivate crops, shape wood, build houses, dig wells, and do many other things. It would also have been easier to protect oneself from wild animals or aggressive neighbours. Nevertheless, it is probable that change did not happen suddenly; at first iron must have been scarce and in some areas it might have remained so for a long time. Thus at the site of Daima, in the north-east of Nigeria, the earliest occurrence of iron was about 500 years later than at Taruga, less than 900 kilometres away. Moreover, even when iron was readily available, it did not mean that people always used it. At Aksum, for instance, in a society with long-established metallurgical skills, stone artefacts were still being used for carving ivory and wood less than 2000 years ago. Poverty, conservatism, superstition, even preference, there are many reasons why people might continue using technologically obsolete tools. Little wonder that iron-smelting took some centuries to reach southern Africa, only reaching its limits in that direction about 1500 years ago.

The adoption of iron by African societies was perhaps the most important technological change that ever occurred in the continent. Although its origins remain uncertain and although its impact was variable in space and time, it nevertheless changed Africa for ever. It not only gave those who used it a technical advantage but also economic, ritual and political power. This was the power of metal and the people of Africa would never be the same again.

10

ANCIENT EGYPT

3000 years of achievement

One of the world's earliest urban civilizations, and one of Africa's most successful, arose in the north-east corner of the African continent, along the banks of the lower River Nile. The ancient state of Egypt, enduring from about 5000 to about 2000 years ago, was remarkable for its long survival, perhaps longer than that of any other state in human history. It was also remarkable for its other achievements, particularly in art, architecture, engineering and scholarly activity. Because it is the oldest example of emerging social complexity in Africa, it is particularly important to try to understand the reason for such success. Fortunately, the extraordinarily rich archaeological and documentary evidence that has survived in Egypt's dry environment provides detailed information about its ancient society. It is also possible to trace the roots of that society amongst the farming people who lived along the lower Nile between about 6500 and about 5000 years ago (Chapter 7). By about 5500 years ago there were already large settlements at Hierakonpolis and other places in southern Egypt, that formed the basis of subsequent social and political development.

Ancient Egypt, much like modern Egypt, consisted of desert. In most places there was little rainfall, in some areas none at all. But Egypt had the Nile, one of the world's great rivers, fed with water from the Ethiopian mountains and from deep in equatorial Africa. Once a year, usually without fail, the Nile flooded a narrow strip of land on each side of it and other nearby low-lying areas. This not only saturated the ground but left a deposit of fertile silt lying on top of it. Each year, after the floodwaters had gone down, large crops of wheat and barley and vegetables could be grown on the irrigated land on each side of the Nile and in the Nile Delta where the river entered the Mediterranean Sea. In addition, substantial flocks of sheep and goats and herds of cattle and pigs were raised. Egypt was (and still is) the gift of the Nile, and the Nile was the gift of Africa. Without the Nile there would have been only desert, with the Nile there was abundant agricultural production that could yield a large surplus to support a complex society with a dense population. There were government officials, priests, craftsmen, artists, scribes, soldiers, merchants and many others, as well as the numerous

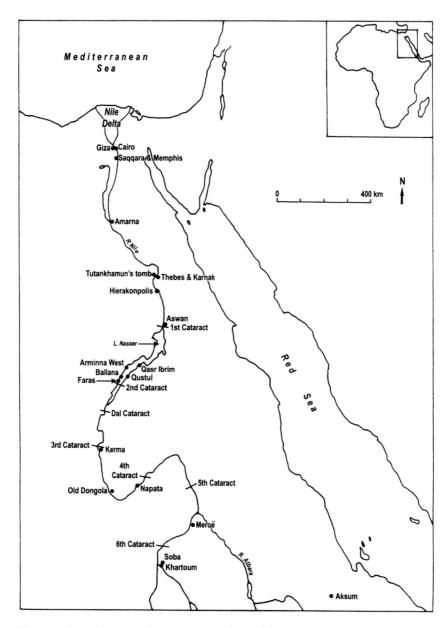

Figure 23 Sites in Ancient Egypt and Nubia. Refer to Chapters 10 and 11. Map by Sue Singleton.

farmers who produced the food. In addition, the Nile provided a means of transportation from one end of this long narrow country to the other. With the prevailing wind blowing from the north and the river flowing from the south, boats could sail in one direction and drift or be rowed back. In this way all sorts of bulky commodities and heavy raw materials could be moved and relatively easy communications could be maintained between different communities.

With plentiful food in most years and often with a substantial surplus, Ancient Egypt was a land of plenty and, moreover, one with a good transportation system that enabled an efficient distribution of resources. Yet each side of the narrow occupied area, usually so close that you could see it from the banks of the Nile itself, there was the desert, shutting this land of plenty off from the outside world. Also the Mediterranean Sea to the north and rocky cataracts in the Nile to the south for a long time protected Egypt from those directions. As time went on the Ancient Egyptians did develop many trading contacts with their southern neighbours along the Nile and with people in Palestine and Syria. However, at first the isolation of Egypt and the agricultural productivity supported by the River Nile appears to have convinced the Egyptians that their land was the very best part of the world and that any change to this situation must be avoided. In short, the Ancient Egyptians were a conservative people, although their society did actually change quite a lot over the centuries.

For much of its history Ancient Egypt was ruled by an absolute monarch, the Pharaoh, who was thought to be the incarnation of the sun-god Ra, the counterpart of Osiris the god of the dead. Thus he possessed both secular and sacred authority and he was central to the maintenance and extension of power that was essential for the survival of the Egyptian state. It was the pharaohs who had unified the many different communities of Egypt about 5000 years ago, and it was they who continued to hold Egyptian society together and to see to it that the Egyptian concept of right order prevailed. Many pharaohs were extremely powerful, although this power declined at times, particularly during the periods known to historians as the First, Second and Third Intermediate Periods. Some pharaohs were literally worshipped, and when they died or, as was believed, returned to being part of the god from which they had come, enormous labour and expense was devoted to making them suitable tombs. Thus, some of the earlier pharaohs were buried in huge stone pyramids, such as those at Giza and Saqqara near Cairo. The largest of these contained well over 2 million blocks of stone, some of them weighing an estimated 15 tonnes each, but it was nevertheless built to fine limits of accuracy. Later pharaohs were buried in a series of chambers cut out of solid rock beneath the ground but their tombs were remarkable for their contents of numerous impressive personal possessions. Such a tomb was that of the Pharaoh Tutankhamun, which was discovered some 80 years ago and has become famous. So important were the pharaohs

Figure 24 Two of the pyramids at Giza.

to them, that the Egyptian people recorded their history in terms of the reigns and dynasties of their rulers. Conventionally, this long stretch of time has been presented as a sequence of periods lasting from about 5000 years ago to about 2000 years ago. They comprise the Early Dynastic Period, the Old Kingdom, the Middle Kingdom, the New Kingdom and the Late Period, the second and subsequent of these being separated from each other by the three Intermediate Periods already referred to. This sequence provides us with the longest and most detailed account of the past in the African continent.

The pharaohs were assisted in their task by a large number of government officials who looked after such matters as the collection of taxes, the construction of irrigation canals and dykes, the maintenance of law and order, the organization of the army, the observation of religious ceremonies, and so on. The existence of such a complicated public service was made possible because there were relatively large numbers of people who were trained to read and write and to understand arithmetic. One of the reasons for the Ancient Egyptians' success for such a long time was, in fact, their invention of a form of writing all their own. At first and subsequently for ceremonial purposes they used a form of picture writing, in which symbols represented sounds, known as hieroglyphs but they also developed more rapid ways of writing for day-to-day purposes, such as hieratic and the later demotic. This ability to write things down allowed the Egyptians to develop a complex government structure and to make great achievements in both science and literature. They were greatly assisted in these matters by their manufacture of a form of paper made from the papyrus reeds that grew along the River Nile and in the Nile Delta. The dry climate of Egypt has preserved many pieces of this material on which the writing can still be read. They show that there was an abundant literature in both prose and poetry and demonstrate an extensive knowledge particularly of astronomy and medicine. For example, the Ancient Egyptians worked out a calendar of 365 days based on the sun, used splints and casts on broken bones, and sewed up open wounds. In addition, inscriptions on the walls of buildings and tombs provide further information about Ancient Egyptian society, especially about history and religion.

The central role of religion in the life of the country also contributed importantly to Ancient Egypt's long survival, by encouraging social and political cohesion. The Egyptians worshipped a whole series of distinctive gods, of which Ra, Amun, Horus, Osiris and Isis were amongst the more important but there was great complexity in their religious ideas, in which there were also changes as time went on. Furthermore, the practices of ordinary people often differed from those of the state religion. Nevertheless, religious observance was vitally important to Ancient Egyptians. The gods had given them the River Nile, its annual flood, and the agricultural abundance that resulted from it. Therefore, the gods must be properly honoured if years of low river levels or excessive flooding were to be prevented. Consequently, much effort and expense went into building temples, often of enormous size, great beauty and impressive technology, such as those of Karnak near Thebes. Most temples were built in stone and the Ancient Egyptians became expert in constructing buildings in this way, the remains of many of them surviving to this day. Not only do they demonstrate architectural and artistic skills but many of them also have carvings or associated sculptures which are informative about Ancient Egyptian life and beliefs.

Mud brick was used for construction as well as stone and there were palaces, houses and other buildings in cities such as Memphis, Thebes and Amarna, as well as humbler dwellings in numerous towns and villages. However, a lot of effort does seem to have been spent on monumental religious buildings. Similarly, a great deal of labour and expense went into the construction of tombs, not only for the pharaohs and their important officials but, at a less ambitious level, for ordinary people as well. The Egyptians' religious beliefs convinced them that there was a life after death and that the deceased must therefore be buried in a tomb furnished with everything necessary for that life. Thus tombs were equipped with furniture and clothing, supplies of food and drink, models showing all manner of daily activities, and so on, depending on what could be afforded. For the same reason, the Egyptians attempted to preserve the dead body by chemical treatment and careful bandaging. Many of the mummies that resulted have survived to the present time, enabling modern researchers to investigate

Figure 25 Middle Kingdom tomb model of a peasant ploughing with oxen, 43 centimetres long. John Pratt after Stead, M. 1986. *Egyptian life.* British
Museum, London, front cover.

diseases and injuries from which Ancient Egyptians suffered. In some
instances, it is even possible to identify a person who died over 3000 years
ago, as in the case of the important pharaoh Rameses II. Because of the
Ancient Egyptians' belief in the afterlife, the contents of their tombs and the
paintings that often decorate tomb walls are a rich source of information
about their lives and beliefs, although often somewhat idealized.

In conclusion, the remarkable survival of the Ancient Egyptian state
resulted from a number of factors: the large agricultural surplus usually produced by the floodwaters of the River Nile, the centralized rule of many of
the pharaohs, the existence of numerous literate government officials, and
the obsession of Ancient Egyptians with religion and with the maintenance
of the existing order. The outcome of these and other related matters was a
long-lasting human culture of great individuality, which maintained social
and economic stability over substantial periods and was able to restore it
after interludes of political breakdown. The success of Ancient Egypt is
impressive but it was also that very success that led eventually to its decline.
Its conservatism made social and political change difficult and contributed
to the periods of instability. Its self-confidence led it into imperial adven-
tures beyond its protective borders, that eventually brought it into conflict
with powerful enemies armed with iron weapons that were superior to those
of bronze on which Egypt still depended. Furthermore, first Greek and then

Roman domination of the eastern Mediterranean resulted in the loss of Egyptian independence, as its grain surplus became a basis of regional power. Subsequently the spread of Christianity and later of Islam, as well as the arrival of immigrants from Arabia and elsewhere, brought about still more changes in Egyptian society, so that the world of the pharaohs was almost forgotten. Until that is the last two centuries or so, when scholars discovered how to read Ancient Egyptian writings and how to reconstruct the life of 5000 to 2000 years ago from the remains of the tombs, temples and other buildings and from the countless objects made at that time.

11

NUBIA

A meeting place of different people

Although it was such an important African development, it seems that Ancient Egypt had relatively little influence on the rest of the African continent. The immensity of the Sahara Desert to its west and the harsh environment of the land to its east isolated Egypt to a large extent. Yet there was one part of Africa with which the Ancient Egyptians and their successors did have frequent contact and where local people reacted by developing their own distinctive cultures. This was Nubia, the land along the River Nile to the south of Egypt, stretching from Aswan in the south of the modern state of Egypt to around Khartoum, the capital of the modern state of the Sudan.

Nubia is the land of the Nile Cataracts, a series of rocky stretches of the river which boats can only pass with difficulty if at all. Like Egypt, in many places settlement is restricted to a narrow strip each side of the river, but further south the surrounding desert gives way to savanna country where flocks of sheep and goats or herds of cattle can be grazed at least during and for a while after the brief wet season. Also, at times in the past the climate was less dry than it is at present. As a result the area has a long history of human settlement and because of its access to such resources as gold and other minerals, ivory, slaves, aromatic substances and other tropical products, it first attracted the attention of the Ancient Egyptians as long as 4000 years ago.

At first as traders, then as conquerors and, for a time, colonizers, the Ancient Egyptians had a considerable impact on Nubia, although that impact was less the further south they went. Also there were periods when internal problems in Ancient Egypt itself reduced or even terminated Egyptian activity in Nubia. Nevertheless, Egyptian colonies grew up in some parts of Nubia and the remains of temples and other buildings of Egyptian style can be found far to the south of Egypt itself. This meant that considerable interaction took place with the native people of Nubia who in turn developed their own cities and forms of government.

Earliest of these was Kerma, in the northern Sudan. Situated on the east bank of the Nile, a substantial urban settlement grew up here by about 3500 years ago. Using bronze tools and herding domesticated animals and cultivating cereals, its inhabitants benefited from substantial trading connections with the Ancient Egyptians. Their settlement consisted of houses of various sizes, suggesting a society in which some people were wealthier and more important than others. A large circular building within the settlement may have been a meeting place for the leaders of society or an audience chamber for its ruler, and the remains of several huge mud brick buildings indicate the existence of a powerful religion. Kerma was enclosed by defensive walls, and evidence from numerous burial mounds nearby, some of the larger of which contained the burials of important people accompanied by hundreds of others who had been sacrificed, suggests that its inhabitants were ruled by a king. It also seems likely that his rule extended over parts of the area around Kerma, where similar sites have been found. Indeed, Kerma may have become one of Africa's earliest states.

Kerma was eventually taken over by the Ancient Egyptians, with whom it had traded so successfully. However, other similar developments followed, first at Napata, further south along the Nile, and then at Meroë, still further south. Napata is the name given to a whole group of sites, consisting of both settlements and cemeteries and dating from a little less than 3000 years ago. The influence of Ancient Egypt was so strong in this area that the inhabitants built small-scale versions of the Egyptian pyramids and temples of Egyptian style, as well as using Egyptian hieroglyphs in their inscriptions. Nevertheless, Napata was the centre of an emerging African state that became known as Kush. So powerful did it become that for about 100 years its rulers also became the pharaohs of Egypt as well.

A little more than 2000 years ago the capital of Kush moved to Meroë, where a city of considerable importance grew up on the east side of the Nile. By this time its Nubian inhabitants were doing things in their own way rather than in the Egyptian way. They constructed buildings of a distinctive style, followed their own religion and developed their own form of writing. Their economy was based on herding and cereal cultivation and they used tools and weapons of iron. Large heaps of slag at Meroë and other places

Figure 26 Rural life in Nubia. Part of an engraving on a Meroitic bronze bowl from Karanog, in southern Egypt. After Woolley, C.L. and Randall-MacIver, D. 1910. *Karanòg: the Romano-Nubian cemetery,* Eckley B. Coxe Junior Expedition to Nubia, Vol. 4, University Museum, University of Pennsylvania, Philadelphia, Plate 27.

indicate that iron-smelting was an important activity. They also made fine pottery, produced textiles of both cotton and wool, practised a range of other handicrafts and created a distinctive art style of their own. It is their buildings that have left the most impressive evidence, however, constructed in fine stonework, in fired brick and in mud brick. The remains of some of their temples and tombs still stand after 2000 years, and excavations have revealed traces of palaces and houses both in Meroë and in other places within the extensive Meroitic state.

The Meroitic state, which controlled not only the valley of the Nile but also parts of the savanna and desert on its margins, was ruled by a king but his queen was also powerful and women sometimes ruled in their own right. Surviving inscriptions record the names of these rulers and although Meroitic writing is not now fully understood, it is apparent that they were both autocratic and divine. At Meroë itself there was a large palace complex enclosed by a wall, within the city, and members of the royal family and other important people were still buried under small pyramids which imitated those of Ancient Egypt but differed in both size and design. However, both burials and settlements indicate that the population mainly consisted of less wealthy people, the majority being hardworking farmers, herdsmen and craftsmen of various kinds.

At its northern end Nubia was in direct contact with Egypt, which during the Greek and subsequently Roman domination of the eastern Mediterranean became increasingly part of what was then one of the centres of world development. At its southern end Nubia reached deep into the heart of tropical Africa. Because the Sahara Desert for a long time made communication so difficult between Mediterranean North Africa and the rest of the continent, Nubia provided the easiest route by which Greek and Roman communities could be supplied with the gold, ivory, slaves, incense, wild animal skins, live animals, ostrich eggs and feathers, ebony, semi-precious stones and other exotic commodities that they desired and which Africa could provide. Transport by water was possible along most of the Nile and, where cataracts prevented this or made it difficult, land routes were developed which also provided short-cuts across the larger bends in the river's course. Land transport seems to have relied on donkeys but as time went on camels may also have been used, although it was only much later that they became so important. Some scholars have called Nubia the 'corridor to Africa' but from an African point of view it was a corridor to Europe and South-West Asia.

The result was that trade seems to have been of major importance to the Meroitic state and was probably the main source of its wealth, particularly for its rulers and their supporters. In exchange for the African products and commodities going north, a variety of manufactured and luxury goods came south. Fine metalwork and glassware have been found at Meroitic sites and it is apparent that large quantities of Egyptian wine and probably also olive oil and honey were imported. Perhaps the most remarkable demonstration of the importance of this trade is a fine bronze head of the Roman emperor Augustus, of Roman manufacture, that was found at the city of Meroë itself. It is significant that, a little over 1500 years ago, the Meroitic state seems to have faded away at the very time that the late Roman world to its north was experiencing a succession of economic and political crises that led to a decline in trade. Also by that time the development of shipping routes along the Red Sea coast had diverted much of the trade with the African interior, so that instead of Nubia it passed through the state of Aksum high in the Ethiopian Highlands (Chapter 12).

Following the decline of the Meroitic state, other important groups emerged in Nubia, such as those whose rulers and leading people were buried in richly equipped tombs at Ballana and Qustul in northern Nubia. Then, after about 1500 years ago, Christianity penetrated the area and several Christian states emerged, of which Makouria and Alwa were the most important. Although Meroë itself seems to have been abandoned, other towns and cities grew up in which churches and cathedrals were built. One of these settlements whose remains have been excavated is known as Arminna West and is situated in northern Nubia on the west bank of the Nile. Another at Faras, in the same area, had a cathedral on whose walls were brightly coloured paintings depicting Christ, the Madonna and Child, and other Christian subjects, as well as Nubian kings, bishops and high-ranking government officials.

One of the most informative sites, however, has been that of the city of Qasr Ibrim in southern Egypt. This was situated at the top of a rocky hill high above the east bank of the Nile, although this is now an island at the edge of the artificial Lake Nasser created in recent times by the construction of the Aswan High Dam. Occupied from Napatan times, about 2500 years ago, until about 200 years ago, Qasr Ibrim has provided a valuable insight into life in northern Nubia over this long period of time. This is particularly so because the site is situated in a part of Nubia where it virtually never rains and such dry conditions have preserved organic substances such as wood, clothing, basketry, grain, rope, paper and other things that would normally not survive. In the course of its long existence, Qasr Ibrim was at different periods an important fortress, even for a short time in the hands of the Romans for whom it was their most southerly base in Africa. At other times it was a Christian pilgrim centre, with a large cathedral, and for centuries it was a thriving commercial and manufacturing community.

Qasr Ibrim was in the north of Nubia but there were also flourishing cities further to the south during the Christian period. At Old Dongola, the capital of the kingdom of Makouria, in what is now the Sudan, at least some of its citizens must have been particularly wealthy because one house had a heated bathroom with piped hot water and painted decorations, whilst elsewhere at this site fragments of pottery toilet seats have been found. Even in

Figure 27 Urban life in Nubia. Ruins of the city of Qasr Ibrim, in southern Egypt. Seen here in recent times, almost surrounded by the waters of Lake Nasser. The large building at its centre was the Christian cathedral.

the far south of Nubia at Soba, the capital of the kingdom of Alwa, situated near the modern city of Khartoum, there is evidence of palatial buildings and of churches.

After about 500 years ago even more changes took place in Nubia, as the Christian religion was gradually replaced by Islam and more and more Arab people moved into the area. In the process, culture and political organization changed yet again. However, this was merely a continuation of the sort of things that had been happening in Nubia for many centuries. This had long been a meeting place of different people, where the original inhabitants mixed with others who came to trade, to conquer, to convert, or to settle. A good demonstration of this has been provided by the inscriptions and manuscripts found at Qasr Ibrim, where the dry conditions have preserved so many of them. Different ones are written in Egyptian hieroglyphs, Demotic, Meroitic, Old Nubian, Latin, Greek, Coptic, Arabic and Turkish. They demonstrate very clearly the varied influences that penetrated this part of Africa along the Nile Valley.

12

AKSUM

A trading metropolis on the Ethiopian Plateau

Almost 2000 years ago, high on the Ethiopian Plateau in north-eastern Africa, there was a thriving city that was the capital of a powerful state. Both city and state were called Aksum and the people of the area were governed by a king, whose subjects included a wealthy elite, priests, scribes, merchants, numerous craftsmen, soldiers, farmers, labourers, and probably slaves. This was a society with a number of urban centres, its own form of writing, coinage in gold, silver and bronze, stone buildings of a distinctive design, unique public monuments, a sophisticated material culture, extensive trading interests both overseas and within Africa, and an important role in international politics. It was also one of the first states in the world to adopt the Christian religion. For perhaps 500 years it flourished and then seems to have died away. So how did this happen: what brought about its remarkable success and what caused its disappearance?

The area that was controlled by Aksum consisted mainly of the north-eastern part of the highlands of Ethiopia, much of it 2000 metres or more above sea-level and now divided between the modern states of Ethiopia and Eritrea. With a generally favourable climate, a range of environments at different heights, and some areas of fertile soils, this was an agriculturally productive land. Farming had developed here some thousands of years previously, based on introduced wheat and barley but also on the locally domesticated cereal teff and other plants, as well as on large numbers of cattle, sheep and goats. Terracing and irrigation were practised and ox-drawn ploughs were used, the only ones in tropical Africa until recent times. In addition, donkeys and mules were used for transport in the often difficult landscape. Aksum's economic base appears to have been a sound one, and one capable of producing a storable surplus that could support both its government and other members of society who were not engaged in farming.

Aksum had other advantages, however. Its geographical position within the African continent enabled it to obtain a variety of raw materials from a wide range of sources. To the west and north-west it could reach the lands of the Nile, to the south and south-west the equatorial regions, to the north-

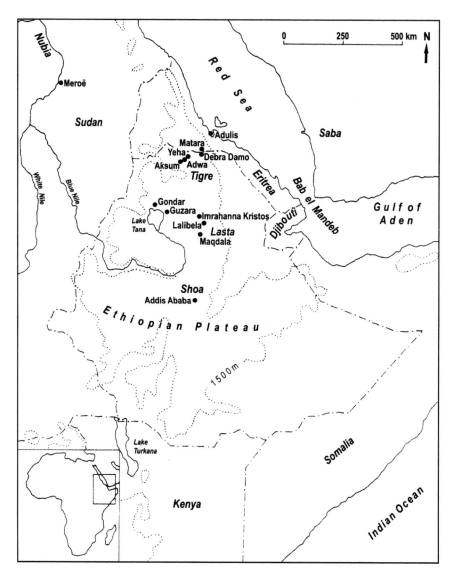

Figure 28 Sites and regions in Aksumite and Christian Ethiopia. Modern political boundaries are also shown. Refer to Chapters 12 and 13. Map by Sue Singleton.

east and south-east the coastal plains of the Red Sea and the Indian Ocean. The extent to which it tapped the resources of all these regions is unknown but it is apparent that it was able to obtain such important commodities as ivory, gold, aromatics, animal skins, salt, copper, iron, slaves, and other things, from a wide area. In addition, Aksum was within a relatively short distance of the narrow straits of the Bab el Mandeb, that separated Africa from the Asian continent. On the other side of those straits, in what is now Yemen and part of Saudi Arabia, lay a similar environment and it seems that there had been contact with the people of that land for many centuries. Indeed, the origins of Aksumite culture between 2000 and 3000 years ago, in a period known to archaeologists as the Pre-Aksumite, were partly a result of such contact. The manner in which this occurred is uncertain but it is significant that the earliest form of writing in north-east Ethiopia used the language and script of the kingdom of Saba on the other side of the Red Sea. Other signs of influence from the same source are evident in Pre-Aksumite stone sculpture, building design and religion. Similarly, the beginnings of urban growth in north-east Ethiopia may also have been stimulated by Sabaean example. Most notable is the evidence from Yeha, principal of which is the ruin of a temple of beautifully finished stonework, that still stands to a height of about 9 metres and dates to about 2500 years ago, contemporary with the Parthenon in Athens.

Aksumite culture seems to have developed out of the Pre-Aksumite but the relationship between the two is not well understood because of a lack of evidence from about 2000 years ago, when Aksum must have been at an important developmental stage. For a knowledge of what then happened we are mainly reliant on archaeology, although ancient Greek and Roman written sources do endorse the general picture. Ethiopian oral traditions are less useful for this early period, except perhaps for the story of the visit of the Queen of Sheba to King Solomon and the consequent birth of the founder of the Ethiopian royal house. This is perhaps a further indication of the importance of influences from across the Red Sea. In addition, we have a number of Aksumite inscriptions on stone written in Ge'ez, the local language at that time, and in the Ethiopian alphabet. Writing on Aksumite coins, either in Ge'ez or in Greek, is also informative, particularly about the succession of Aksumite kings and the dates that they ruled. It is nevertheless archaeological evidence that tells us most about ancient Aksum.

Best known of this evidence is that from Aksum itself, where substantial remains are still above ground or have been excavated in recent times. Particularly interesting are tall, thin standing stones, known to archaeologists as 'stelae', that apparently marked the locations of burials of important individuals. The majority of these are plain stones a few metres in height, often with quite rough surfaces, but in the centre of Aksum stood a group of much larger ones that had been carefully carved to represent multi-storeyed buildings, complete with windows and a door. Originally there were six of

Figure 29 The largest of the stelae still standing at Aksum. It is a single piece of stone weighing about 150 tonnes, 21 metres in height, and carved to represent a nine-storeyed building. Reproduced by permission of David Phillipson.

these, of which three were literally monstrous in size. One of them still stands, a single block of hard stone weighing about 150 tonnes and 21 metres high, with another 3 metres below ground. It is carved to represent nine storeys. Two others which fell long ago were larger, the biggest being about 500 tonnes in weight and nearly 33 metres in length, so massive that it is thought that it fell whilst being erected. These 'storeyed stelae' seem to date to just before the adoption of Christianity, about 1700 years ago, and appear to have been funerary ideals of the stone buildings in which royalty and members of the elite lived. These buildings, remains of which have been excavated both in and around Aksum and at the urban site of Matara, consisted of complexes of square courtyards and towers of two or perhaps three storeys in height, set on a solid masonry base. Consisting mainly of mud-bonded rubble reinforced with timber in a distinctive Aksumite way, it is doubtful if such buildings could ever have been truly multi-storeyed. However, ideas about life after death must have offered no such limits and the storeyed stelae were perhaps meant to express this, as well as being intended to generate admiration for the person commemorated.

Associated with the storeyed stelae are several underground tombs, the most important being a complex of stone-built chambers known to archaeologists as the 'Mausoleum' and an extensive rock-cut tomb now called the 'Tomb of the Brick Arches'. Elsewhere in both Aksum and its neighbourhood are other stone-built and rock-cut tombs, most of them clearly intended for the burial of important individuals, in some cases almost certainly royalty. Other tombs, particularly those of the 'Gudit Stelae Field' south-west of Aksum, seem to have been for people of lesser status but in many cases still wealthy enough to afford rougher stelae as grave-markers. Clearly this was a stratified society, with the king at the top of the social pyramid and farmers, labourers and probably slaves at the bottom. Archaeological excavations and field surveys have also begun to shed light on how those lower classes lived, in roughly built thatched houses of stone or mud, many of them in rural villages and hamlets. It is these people who would have formed the labour force of Aksumite society and it is also they who would have provided most of the warriors whenever there was a war.

In between the social elite and the labouring mass there must have been a whole range of craftsmen and specialist workers. Aksumite material culture was sophisticated and diverse, demonstrating the existence of a wide variety of skills and substantial technological knowledge. Stone was quarried, transported in large pieces, carved, erected as stelae, used extensively in building, and sometimes inscribed. Water-storage dams were constructed, as well as terracing and irrigation systems. The manufacture and use of fired bricks and lime mortar were understood, and how to employ these materials in brick arches and brick barrel-vaulting. Large quantities of pottery were made, without the use of a potter's wheel but nevertheless often of high quality. Metallurgical expertise included the working of gold, silver, copper and bronze, and iron. An impressive range of relevant processes was understood, including smelting, forging, welding, riveting, production of plate, drilling, perforating, casting, polishing, plating (both annealing and mercury-gilding), enamelling, and the striking of coins. Ivory was carved and lathe-turned with great skill, leather was worked and probably textiles were manufactured. Wine was made from grapes and glass-working was carried out, most likely using imported glass as the raw material.

Imports, indeed, made a substantial contribution to Aksumite life, particularly to that of the more wealthy. As already explained, the location of Aksum and its kingdom must have enabled it to tap a range of raw materials from deep within the African continent. However, that same location also allowed it to participate in the maritime trade of the Red Sea which, significantly, was flourishing at the very time that Aksum was so successful. The Aksumite port of Adulis, only eight days' journey from Aksum itself, became the gateway through which a stream of imports and exports passed. In particular, the late classical world of the Mediterranean was hungry for the exotic products of the African interior, and the Aksumites in turn seem to have developed a remarkable appetite for the sophisticated manufactures of that world. Using both archaeological and historical sources it is possible to reconstruct the list of exports and imports. Going out were ivory, gold, obsidian, emeralds, aromatic substances, rhinoceros horn, hippopotamus teeth and hide, tortoiseshell, slaves, and monkeys and other live animals. Coming in were iron and other metals, and things made of them, glass and ceramic items, fabrics and clothing, wine and sugar-cane, vegetable oils, aromatic substances and spices. As was so often to be the case with African external trade, this was basically one involving an exchange of raw materials and primary products for manufactures and value-added commodities.

This participation in what was one of the major world trade routes, reaching from the Mediterranean to the Indian Ocean, greatly increased Aksum's wealth. With wealth came power, so that Aksumite political authority at times extended across the Red Sea to the Yemeni highlands and perhaps westwards as far as the Nile Valley. It was, it seems, the increasing importance of Aksum's role as a supplier to the outside world of African commodities, that contributed to the decline of Meroë (Chapter 11), as that trade moved away from the Nile Valley to the Red Sea. The extent of Aksumite overseas contacts is indeed impressive, as indicated by Aksumite gold coins found in Yemen and India and by Indian coins found in north-east Ethiopia. Moreover, those Aksumite gold coins were clearly minted expressly for the international trade, inscribed in Greek as they were and with their weight apparently based on standards employed in the eastern Roman Empire. In contrast, Aksumite silver and bronze coins were inscribed in Ge'ez and seem to have had a largely internal circulation.

It all came to an end, quite when is not entirely clear, although a date a

Figure 30 Aksumite copper coin of King Armah, who reigned almost 1400 years ago. Left: the king enthroned holding a processional cross. Right: reverse of the coin showing a cross with a gold inlay. Reproduced by permission of David Phillipson.

little over 1300 years ago seems most likely. As to the cause, two factors might have been responsible. First, over-exploitation that brought on environmental deterioration, resulting in a scarcity of timber and in soil erosion that led to a reduction in agricultural productivity. Second, the rapid extension of Islamic control over the Red Sea trade, which effectively cut off Christian Aksum's access to its most important markets. Overseas trade had not caused the rise of Aksum but undoubtedly it had contributed to Aksum's ultimate prosperity, and its fairly abrupt termination almost certainly accelerated an economic and political collapse that might already have been imminent.

13

CHURCH AND STATE

Survival in Ethiopia

The Aksumite state seems to have declined and disappeared sometime between about 1300 and 1000 years ago. It appears that the loss of the Red Sea trade and environmental deterioration in the Aksum region led to a change in the economic basis of society. Probably the control of productive land became more important than the procurement and exchange of trading commodities; consequently the political centre of Ethiopia moved south into areas with a greater rainfall. Subsequently it shifted frequently within those areas, and the extent of its territories varied greatly from one period to another, but the Ethiopian state endured. Partly this was because of a mountainous landscape that discouraged external aggressors, partly it was because of a distinctive set of cultures, but mainly it was because of the powerful belief of Ethiopian people in their own particular form of the Christian faith. Their church supported the state, which in turn supported the church. It was this alliance of church and state that ensured the survival of Ethiopia until modern times, however much its fortunes fluctuated. Indeed, Ethiopia was one of the very few parts of Africa that was never successfully colonized by Europeans.

Like Aksum before it (Chapter 12), Christian Ethiopia was in part a literate society but the earliest surviving well-dated documents, written in Ge'ez, are only about 700 years old and Ethiopian writing was for a long time mainly concerned with religious matters. Those historical accounts that do exist were often written long after the events that they described and were sometimes influenced by political considerations. Oral traditions, although plentiful, are often difficult to interpret. Nevertheless, it is possible to piece together an outline of Ethiopian history over the last 1000 years or so since the Aksumite state faded away. For the earlier periods the picture is indistinct but it becomes clearer as the present is approached, because of increasingly frequent visits by outsiders who left accounts of their experiences. From these various sources, it appears that the decline of Aksum was followed by a period of unrest, which the traditions attribute to a queen called Gudit. However, by at least 900 years ago there emerged the Zagwe dynasty of rulers, who were centred on the Lasta district, almost 300

76

kilometres south-east of Aksum. Several of the Zagwe rulers were great church builders and it is to the best known of them, Lalibela, that tradition attributes the rock-cut churches of Lalibela, a place named after him. Then, about 700 years ago, the centre of political power shifted even further south, with the rise of the Solomonic dynasty in the region known as Shoa. Claiming descent from King Solomon and the Queen of Sheba, whose son Menilek had brought the Ark of the Covenant to Aksum, where it is said to be still kept, this was the dynasty to which most Emperors of Ethiopia belonged until recent times. The prevailing theme during this long period was one of survival in the face of a variety of threats: Islamic aggression, Roman Catholic conversion, pastoral immigrants from the south, internal disintegration, and Italian invasions.

The remarkable thing about this period in Ethiopia's history is that there has been so little archaeological research devoted to it. Excavators have focused their attention on earlier periods, such as that of Aksum (Chapter 12). One reason for this is the semi-nomadic life of many of Christian Ethiopia's rulers, particularly before about 500 years ago. They lived in what have been called 'moving capitals', some of which might have contained as many as 100,000 people; vast tent cities that would remain in one place for a few months or years and then shift to a new site. Consisting of the royal court, the ruler's army, government and church officials, merchants, tradesmen, servants, and a variety of other people, not to mention large numbers of mules and horses and other animals, these settlements rapidly depleted the available food, firewood and other resources of their location and their occupants had no choice but to move on. This mobility seems to have been a necessary strategy for the maintenance of large settlements in a region where resources were often thinly spread and the means of transportation limited. It was also, no doubt, an effective way of governing the extensive and difficult terrain of the Ethiopian Highlands. The ruler could control an uncooperative area merely by moving the royal capital there and, if that failed, the royal army would already be at hand to solve the problem.

Over the last 500 years or so, moving capitals began to be replaced by static ones but the location of these also changed frequently and there was a particular tendency for each emperor to have a different capital from his predecessor. Even Gondar, which became a more permanent capital about 350 years ago, was frequently occupied by the ruler and his retinue only during the wet seasons. This was because for most of the rest of the time he was engaged in military expeditions as a means of holding the state together. Nevertheless, by about 200 years ago Ethiopia had effectively disintegrated and during its later reunification the capital moved yet again, eventually becoming fixed at Addis Ababa only a little more than a century ago. In such circumstances, with constantly moving capitals and static ones that often lasted for only brief periods, it is little wonder that archaeologists have been discouraged from excavation. Nevertheless, Christian Ethiopia actually offers one of the most important untapped archaeological research topics in Africa. Although its major settlements were often of short duration, their populations were frequently so large that they must have left substantial cultural evidence, and site locations and dates of occupation are often known, even if only vaguely. At the very least these sites could provide a sequence, from which an archaeological account of the last 1000 years and more could be constructed.

For the present, the physical evidence for Christian Ethiopia is limited to surviving structures and ruins or to other features accessible without excavation. There are a large number of these but the most important are those of a religious character, principally churches and monasteries. These belong to the Ethiopian Orthodox Church, a relative of the Egyptian Coptic Church which until recent times provided its head. One of the first Christian buildings was probably the Cathedral of Maryam Tsion, at Aksum, perhaps originally built during the Aksumite period but with a surviving structure only some 450 years old. Aksum seems to have been one of the few settlements that was continuously occupied throughout the Christian Ethiopian period, having become a city that was sacred to Ethiopian Christians and to which those emperors who were able to do so went for their coronation. However, the earliest surviving church is probably that of Debra Damo, also in the Tigre region, which might be as much as 1000 years old. This is part of a monastery situated on a flat summit surrounded by vertical cliffs, the only access being by rope. The church displays the same distinctive construction techniques that characterized the Aksumite buildings of earlier times, and these continued to be used for many centuries in numerous Ethiopian churches. Nevertheless, the form and layout of some churches show influences from Syria and Nubia, both areas with which Christian Ethiopia had early contact.

Among the more remarkable churches is that of Imrahanna Kristos, in the Lasta district, which was built inside a cave almost 900 years ago. Other churches were also constructed inside caves but churches that were themselves carved out of rock are far more common, some 200 of them being known in Ethiopia. Many of these are in the form of humanly-made caves and in some cases probably originated as natural caves that were artificially enlarged. Indeed, caves were themselves often adapted as churches. All such churches are very difficult to date but some might be very old. The most developed type could be those that were carved both inside and out from islands of rock isolated by quarrying. This is the form of the most famous rock-cut churches of Ethiopia, the twelve at Lalibela, which according to tradition were all the creation of King Lalibela, almost 800 years ago. However, it seems likely that their carving actually extended over a longer period than his reign and that the whole complex merely took its final form under his direction. The largest of these churches, Medhane Alem, measures 33.5 by 23.5 metres and is 11 metres high. Another, Ghiorghis, has a plan

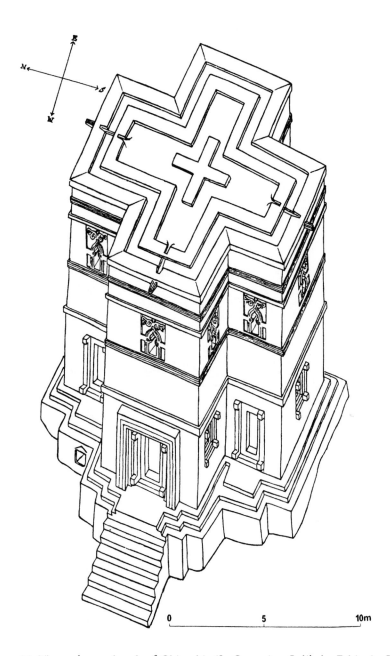

Figure 31 The rock-cut church of Ghiorghis (St George) at Lalibela, Ethiopia. It is carved both outside and inside from a huge piece of solid rock isolated by quarrying. Reproduced by permission of the Society of Antiquaries of London from Buxton, D.R. 1971. The rock-hewn and other medieval churches of Tigré Province, Ethiopia. *Archaeologia* 103, Figure 33.

in the shape of a cross, and is a most impressive example of craftsmanship. Overall, the churches of Christian Ethiopia, both built and rock-cut, provide a vital source of information about the society which produced them. This is not only because they constituted the most significant static element in that society but also because they preserved documents, books, paintings, symbolic objects and traditions that might otherwise not have survived.

About 450 years ago the political centre of Ethiopia shifted yet again, this time to near Lake Tana, the source of the Blue Nile. This is a particularly fertile region with a pleasant climate and it was here that the tendency towards more static capitals became more marked. Although shifts in location within the region continued for almost a century, the capital was eventually fixed at Gondar to the north of the lake and remained there for over 200 years. One consequence of this greater stability was the construction of a series of impressive lime-mortared stone buildings in some of the short-lived capitals and at Gondar itself. Functioning as palaces, these were actually castles built in some cases under Indian or Spanish supervision but uniquely Ethiopian in appearance. The first of them was at Guzara, a rectangular structure measuring 18 by 12 metres set high on a hill. It was of two storeys, with round towers on each of its two northern corners and a square tower at its south-eastern corner. The latter was probably of four storeys, almost 15 metres in height, but by modern times it had collapsed.

It was at Gondar that such buildings became most common. Many emperors, it seems, insisted on their own castle and there are a total of six of them, in a large walled enclosure that also contains several churches and other structures. Oldest and most important of the Gondar castles is that built by the Emperor Fasiladas about 350 years ago, a two-storeyed square structure of about 25 by 25 metres, with conical angle towers and a square tower 32 metres in height. It is probable that this interest in the building of fortifications was a response to the introduction of firearms during the same period. However, Ethiopian rulers were interested in the safety of their souls as well as of their bodies and Gondar has no less than 44 churches. Their building activities also extended to the construction of several bridges in the Lake Tana area, an important contribution to communications.

Christian Ethiopia is better known from its documentary and oral history than from its archaeology but there is abundant physical evidence that has great potential for future archaeological research. Not only do the built and rock-cut churches and the royal castles offer a vital material record of Ethiopia's successful survival but there must also be numerous extensive settlement sites that have never been investigated. The enormous shifting capitals of earlier times surely left discernible traces on the landscape and the amazing churches of Lalibela could hardly have been carved without a large labour force that must have lived close by. For more recent times there are also interesting possibilities, such as the fortress of Maqdala, where almost 150 years ago the Emperor Téwodros II unsuccessfully defied a British army,

Figure 32 The castle of Emperor Fasiladas, in Gondar, Ethiopia, as it was about 140 years ago. From Heuglin, T. von 1874. *Reise nach Abessinien, den Gala-Laendern, Ost-Sudan und Chartum in den Jahren 1861 und 1862.* Griesbach, Gera.

or the battlefield of Adwa, where the soldiers of Menilek II smashed an invading Italian army a little over a century ago. There are, indeed, innumerable ways in which archaeology could shed fresh light on Ethiopia's remarkable survival.

14

OPPORTUNITY AND CONSTRAINT

The Lake Chad story

Lake Chad is the largest African lake north of the equator but it is situated in some of West Africa's driest savanna and to its north lies the Sahara Desert. Indeed, it would not exist without the rivers that flow into its southern end bringing water from areas with greater rainfall. Its climate is markedly seasonal, with a relatively short wet season and a long and increasingly hot dry season. The resulting rainfall is adequate to the south but declines towards the north until it is very low. Consequently, the area around the lake, which is nowadays divided between the countries of Nigeria, Cameroon, Chad and Niger, provides a considerable challenge to human settlement. On the one hand it offers grazing for livestock, land for cereal cultivation and abundant fishing, but on the other it threatens contrasting extremes of both drought and flooding, as well as high temperatures and seasonal absence of surface water and animal feed. In addition, climatic oscillations have further complicated the environment to which people have had to adapt. Thus, so far as human populations have been concerned, the Lake Chad region has been characterized by a complex interplay of opportunity and constraint, an interplay constantly shifting in time and space. The manner in which communities have adapted to these conditions makes a remarkable story, a story that starts at least 8000 years ago and whose details we are still piecing together, mainly from archaeological evidence from Borno in the extreme north-east of Nigeria.

The trouble with Lake Chad is that it will not stand still. During an arid climatic phase between about 20,000 and 12,000 years ago it dried up completely and sand dunes formed in its vicinity. Then the climate grew moister, the lake refilled, and by about 6500 years ago the lake was 40 metres higher than its present level, so that it became a vast inland sea. Subsequently its level fell as conditions again became drier, particularly after about 4000 years ago. However, all these changes were probably complicated by numerous medium-sized and smaller ones, some of them lasting for only short periods. Even within the last 50 years there have been places around the lake that were underwater in one decade, dry two decades later, and once again inundated two decades after that. Given the high tempera-

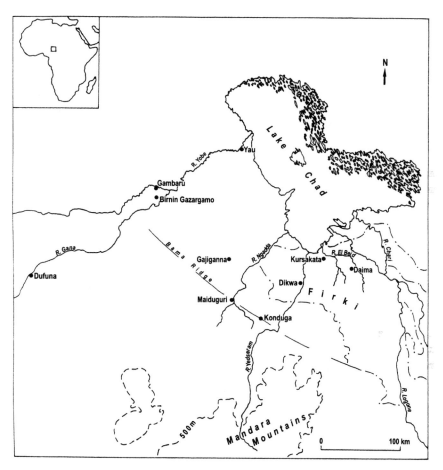

Figure 33 Important sites and places in the Nigerian part of the Lake Chad region. Refer to Chapter 14. Map by Sue Singleton.

tures of the dry season and the seasonal flooding that in many areas follows the short wet season, human populations have had to adapt to a situation where at times they and their livestock had too little water but at other times too much.

Appropriately, the earliest evidence that we have is a boat, an approximately 8000-year-old dugout canoe 8.4 metres long, found buried 5 metres deep in water-laid deposits at Dufuna in the extreme north of Nigeria. It is the oldest boat in Africa and one of the oldest in the world. No artefacts were found with it but at such a date it must have belonged to stone-using people who were fishing and hunting and gathering, probably in a lagoon bordering the much expanded Lake Chad. Its discovery shows how adaptable these earliest-known inhabitants of the region were and suggests a high level of mobility. However, the next indication of human presence in the region is about 1000 years later, by which time people were present on the beach ridge formed by the high lake and separating it from river-fed lagoons to the south-west. The site of Konduga, on what is known as the Bama Ridge, appears to have been occupied by stone-using hunter-gatherers, who used pottery decorated in a similar way to some of the early pottery in the Sahara. The cultural evidence is very limited and no animal bones were found at the site, making it difficult to be sure about the economy of its occupants. Nevertheless, Konduga suggests that the beach ridge formed a land bridge that gave access to both the lake and the lagoons, and from which settlement spread out across the former lake bed as the water level subsequently fell by some 20 metres.

Evidence for such settlement comes from about 120 sites in a former delta between the south-west corner of Lake Chad and the Bama Ridge. The best known of these sites is Gajiganna which is dated from about 3800 to 2800 years ago. At that time the surrounding landscape consisted of slightly raised sandy areas interspersed with clay depressions, many of which held water throughout the year. The Gajiganna people lived in villages, probably of wattle-and-daub houses, and kept cattle, goats and sheep. Their diet included fish, water birds, land and freshwater molluscs, and a number of smaller land mammals. They also collected wild grass seeds and fruits and eventually began cultivating pearl millet. Their technology was based on stone and included distinctive flaked arrowheads similar to some found in the Sahara, as well as ground stone axes, and numerous grindstones presumably for the preparation of plant foods. However, the absence of stone in the lake area made it necessary to obtain supplies from considerable distances and resulted in the manufacture and use of a range of bone artefacts, including barbed harpoons. Finely finished pottery was also made, decorated with mat and comb impressions, as well as small clay figurines of both humans and animals. The dead were buried within the settlement, without any grave goods.

Evidence from Gajiganna suggests that its environment was more attractive to human settlement than it subsequently became, as conditions grew even drier and Lake Chad shrank still further. The consequence of these changes was the abandonment of the Gajiganna sites but at the same time a new area became available for settlement to the south of the lake, a huge area known to its modern inhabitants as the *firki*. Formerly covered by extensive lagoons, this consisted of treeless plains of black clay that baked rock-hard during the dry season but flooded during the brief wet season. Because the clay retained moisture well into the dry season, these plains had considerable potential both for keeping domesticated animals and cultivating crops but there were relatively few places where villages could be built above the seasonal flood levels. These consisted of slightly raised areas that were probably the tops of sand dunes from the earlier arid period, protruding through the later clay deposits. As the *firki* was settled, villages tended to be confined to these areas. Continual occupation, in some cases from about 3000 years ago to the present day, has built up mounds of cultural debris that provide a detailed record of human activity in the area.

Many of these settlement mounds have been identified around the southern end of Lake Chad, extending from north-east Nigeria across northern Cameroon and into Chad. A number have been excavated, the most notable one being at Daima where over 11 metres of deposit were sectioned with a massive trench. Occupation had commenced almost 3000 years ago and continued until less than 500 years ago. The earliest villagers kept cattle and goats but also hunted and fished. They probably collected wild grass seeds and cultivated pearl millet, because evidence for these activities has been found at Kursakata, another settlement mound in the same area. The Daima people used ground stone axes and grindstones but stone had to be brought from great distances and so many of their tools and weapons were made from bone, including barbed harpoons. They made finely finished pottery, often decorated with comb and mat impressions and plaited cord roulettes. They also made small clay figurines, particularly of cattle, and later of humans also. Their houses were probably light structures of wood and grass but as time went on they built in both wattle-and-daub and mud, some of the later buildings having floors made up of pieces of broken pottery set on edge. The dead were buried within the settlement, one individual having died violently with a bone harpoon still embedded in his body.

Amongst the changes that took place during the long occupation of Daima was the introduction of iron about 2000 years ago. Somewhat later, decorative items of copper alloy also appeared and glass and carnelian beads, suggesting the development of wider contacts with the outside world. In addition the pottery changed, with new types of rouletted decoration being adopted, particularly carved roulettes late in the occupation. Also late were some pots that were huge and were perhaps used for brewing beer. Furthermore, sorghum cultivation was adopted at a later date and goats seem to have increased in importance. Finally, socket-stem smoking pipes were

Figure 34 The main excavation at Daima settlement mound, showing a section through about 2500 years of human occupation.

found in the uppermost layers, an African design that was a response to the introduction of tobacco from America about 400 years ago.

By that time some of the settlement mounds of the *firki* seem to have become almost urban and were probably grouped into small early states.

However, many were abandoned about 400 years ago, at a time when documentary records indicate that the Islamic state of Borno was expanding into the region. In time this resulted in changes to the population of the clay plains, as Kanuri people and Shuwa Arab people moved into the formerly Kotoko area. Nevertheless, the economy of the plains remained much the same, based particularly on growing sorghum and keeping cattle and goats. It seems likely that the Borno take-over of the *firki* was at least partly the result of increasingly dry conditions to its north, where between about 500 and 200 years ago the state capital of Birnin Gazargamo was located in the valley of the Yobe River. Excavations at this urban site and at a settlement mound at Yau, occupied from about 1000 to 500 years ago, produced pottery similar to that which appeared in the *firki* only in recent centuries. It was characterized by distinctive nodular rouletting and by patterns incised through a red surface coating on some pottery.

The Borno state, that probably brought together a number of different people as the Kanuri, originated from a ruling group who migrated from Kanem, east of Lake Chad, about 600 years ago, probably because of deteriorating environmental conditions. They brought with them experience in trans-Saharan trade, from which they might have acquired the use of horses, which in Borno gave them a military advantage over their southerly neighbours. Also through their trading contacts, they had already adopted the Islamic faith. By about 400 years ago, continuing trade with North Africa, particularly in slaves, had brought Borno other benefits. These included the making and use of fired bricks, as at the Yobe Valley sites of Birnin Gazargamo and Gambaru, the possession of firearms, and limited literacy. Having expanded into the region to the west and south of Lake Chad, Borno became a powerful state that survived until about 100 years ago. It was then destroyed by Rabeh, a military adventurer from the Sudan, who used Dikwa on the edge of the *firki* as his capital. He in turn was defeated by the expanding forces of European colonialism, as the agents of Britain, Germany and France came face to face in that same crucial *firki* region.

Such is the story of Lake Chad, a story of people learning to live with the lake and adapting not only to its difficult environment but to both the long-term and short-term changes to which it has been prone. There is, perhaps, no better example of the sophisticated human adaptation to the opportunity and constraint of this area than the growing of the dry-season sorghum known as *masakwa* on the black clay plains south of the lake. Sown on the higher areas during the wet season inundation, its seedlings are transplanted into the moist clay as the floods recede after the rains have ended. The crop then grows on the retained moisture in the clay, to be harvested over four months after the end of the rains. It is a remarkable demonstration of how people can succeed even in the face of adversity, which is perhaps the moral of this story, a story that could not have been written prior to the archaeological investigations of the last 40 years.

15

FACING THE MEDITERRANEAN
Carthaginian, Greek and Roman North Africa

North Africa was for a long time part of a world that was separated from the rest of the African continent. Wedged between the Sahara Desert and the Mediterranean Sea, it inevitably looked to the north rather than to the south. To the east its fertile coast was so narrow that in places the desert reached the sea but the coast broadened in the west to include cultivable plains and there were mountains separating it from the desert. Climatically, North Africa belonged with the Mediterranean, with hot dry summers and mild winters when most of the modest rainfall occurred. Culturally, the region formed a meeting place for the peoples of the Levant, Greece and Rome with those of North Africa. As such it played a role in the history of Europe as well as of Africa. Each was to influence the other and the common link was the Mediterranean Sea, providing relatively easy movement for traders and migrants and a frequent focus for armed conflict. A number of sea-oriented colonial settlements grew up in North Africa between about 2800 and 1300 years ago, resulting in complex interaction with the indigenous inhabitants and the development of distinctive literate communities. Towards the end of the period Christianity was widely adopted but was subsequently overwhelmed by Islam, following invasion of the region by Arab people (Chapter 16).

The first outsiders to make their home in North Africa were Phoenician seafarers from cities at the eastern end of the Mediterranean, on the coast of what is now Lebanon. With exceptional skills in shipbuilding and navigation, they gradually developed trade routes throughout the Mediterranean and established coastal trading colonies as far away as south-western Spain, beyond the Strait of Gibraltar. These included a number in present-day western Libya, Tunisia, Algeria and Morocco, in the latter case on its Atlantic as well as its Mediterranean coast. One of these colonies, Carthage, significantly situated at the narrowest part of the Mediterranean between modern Tunisia and Sicily, eventually grew into a major city that controlled much of western North Africa. In addition to extensive trading interests, a highly successful agriculture was developed, in particular producing olive oil, wine, honey and dates, as well as a variety of fruit, the surplus of some of

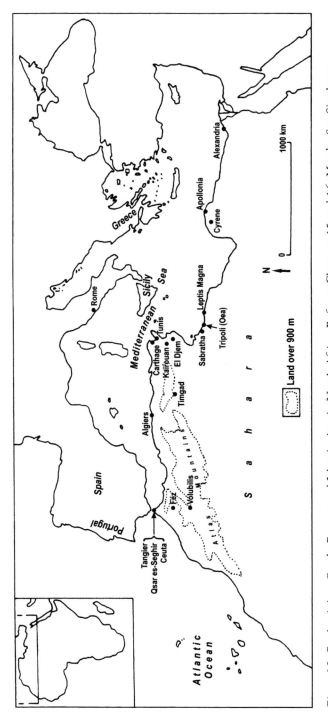

Figure 35 Carthaginian, Greek, Roman and Islamic sites in North Africa. Refer to Chapters 15 and 16. Map by Sue Singleton.

these commodities being exported. With commercial prosperity came increasing political power in the western and central Mediterranean, leading to confrontation on both sea and land with the emerging Roman state. The resulting Punic Wars, three in little over a century, culminated in the destruction of the city of Carthage almost 2150 years ago and the conquest of its territories by the Romans, who later rebuilt the city.

Because of its destruction and subsequent rebuilding, the excavation of the Punic city of Carthage has proved difficult. Nevertheless, it is apparent that the latest phase of its over 600 years of existence was carefully planned, with streets crossing at right angles and stone houses of several storeys. Shops and workplaces seem to have been mixed with the domestic accommodation and the buildings were provided with cisterns and pipes for the supply of water, and soakaways and other pipes for waste water and sanitation. Further information about life in the Punic period has been obtained from burials, including some of young children who might have been the victims of sacrifices that are mentioned in documentary sources. However, in view of its role both in maritime trade and as a sea-power, it is the archaeological investigation of the two interconnected harbours at Carthage that is perhaps most interesting. Enclosed from the sea and entered by a narrow channel, the latest form of these consisted of an outer commercial harbour and an inner military one. On an island in the centre of the latter was a circular stone building providing covered storage for at least 30 warships and up to 140 others could have been berthed around the perimeter of the harbour.

Carthaginian settlement did not extend to the east of what is now western Libya. It was the Greeks who colonized this part of the African coast over 2600 years ago, choosing the region subsequently known as Cyrenaica, to the south of their homeland and easily reached by sea. With a better environment than the coast to either east or west, both agricultural and urban development was possible. The colony exported silphium, an indigenous strong-smelling plant now extinct that was used in Greece and Rome for both culinary and medicinal purposes. Other exports included fine horses, cereals, fruit and even roses. Some of the early settlements eventually grew into major centres, of which the port of Apollonia and the city of Cyrene were the most important. The latter had fine public buildings but never achieved the fame of Alexandria, another Greek city that was situated at the western edge of the Nile delta. The colonists in Cyrenaica maintained strong links with the Greek world to their north but adverse land and sea conditions limited their contact with the Punic colonies to their west. Even after Cyrenaica was taken over by the Romans some 2000 years ago, most of the inhabitants of its cities remained Greek in language and culture.

It was the extension of Roman control over North Africa and Egypt that had the greatest impact on the region. By a little over 2000 years ago the northern edge of the African continent had become the southern edge of the

Roman Empire. As such, for four centuries or more North Africa was an integral part of a huge area with similar political institutions, economic and social organization, and culture. At least officially there was even a common language, in the form of Latin. Much of North Africa seems to have flourished during this period, which has left abundant archaeological evidence, particularly of urban life, as well as documentary evidence. Three of the most important Roman cities were Leptis Magna, Sabratha and Oea, situated in what is now western Libya. Oea is covered by the modern city of Tripoli but the other two places have substantial stone ruins of Roman buildings that have survived to the present and include some of the finest architecture in the Roman Empire. Leptis Magna was larger than Sabratha and contained impressive administrative buildings, several monumental arches, various temples, Christian churches, sumptuous public baths and latrines, a gymnasium, a theatre, an amphitheatre, and a chariot-racing course, as well as two forums, a market, and harbour installations including warehouses and a lighthouse. The city was carefully planned, with paved streets most of which met at right angles. It was supplied with water through underground conduits from a reservoir some 20 kilometres away. Its houses included some remarkably fine ones, that had highly decorative mosaic pavements.

Clearly, Leptis Magna and its two neighbouring cities were wealthy. Apparently they became so on the basis of highly successful agriculture, much of the produce of which was exported to Rome and other cities in the Empire. The most important commodity seems to have been olive oil, that was produced from extensive olive groves in the vicinity, but grain also had a significant role, as did the garum sauce that was made from the entrails of salted fish and considered a great delicacy. In addition, there were trade goods obtained from nomadic desert peoples to the south of the region controlled by the Romans: gold, gemstones, ivory, slaves, and a variety of wild animals that were used in the amphitheatres of Rome and other cities. Although trade with the African interior was probably far less than it later became, it is nevertheless interesting to note the live wild animals that reached Rome from what must have been a variety of sources. They included elephants, lions, leopards, hippopotami, rhinoceros, giraffes, and even zebras.

However, the most important part of the economy of Roman North Africa as a whole was its agriculture, which supported numerous cities, towns, rural settlements, estates and farms, as well as producing a massive surplus for export. Particularly productive was the region which now forms the northern part of Tunisia. South-west of the rebuilt city of Carthage was an extensive wheat-growing district and as time went on the grain shipments to Rome from there and from other parts of North Africa became extremely important. There was also widespread production of olive oil, wine and other farm produce. Consequently, a great deal of wealth was

Figure 36 Roman mosaic at Tabarka, northern Tunisia, depicting a villa on a country estate. From Dunbabin, K.M.D. 1978. *The mosaics of Roman North Africa*. Clarendon Press, Oxford, Plate 112 (source: German Archaeological Institute, Rome).

generated, particularly by large agricultural estates which were often the property of absentee landowners and worked by slaves. There is abundant archaeological evidence for this wealth in cities such as El Djem, in present-day Tunisia, with its massive amphitheatre that could seat 30,000 people and the numerous mosaics recovered from its houses that vividly illustrate both mythology and contemporary life. Perhaps even more indicative of affluence is the sumptuous multi-seater latrine, constantly flushed with running water, in the Seaward Baths at Sabratha. Such facilities needed a sophisticated infrastructure and it appears that the Romans went to considerable lengths to provide this. Given the frequently hot and dry environment of North Africa, water supply was especially important. Roman Carthage, for instance, was supplied with water from some 80 kilometres away, carried by an aqueduct and in places by underground conduits. Rural water-control schemes and irrigation systems are also thought to have been developed at this time, although it seems that some of these were actually of pre-Roman origin. In addition, the Romans built bridges and thousands of kilometres of roads.

All these achievements would not have been possible without adequate security and this was provided by the Roman army, in North Africa's case in the form of the Third Augustan Legion. Its soldiers kept the native population in order and prevented incursions by the desert nomads. To achieve this they built camps and military towns, army veterans from this and other parts of the Empire often retiring to the latter or to farms nearby. It was also the army that built the roads, bridges, water supply systems and even town drains. The most impressive and best preserved amongst the military towns was Timgad, in what is now eastern Algeria, which was laid out with military precision as a rectangular grid of streets and buildings. The army also built and manned a series of forts and lookout posts and dug a number of defensive ditches, to protect the long desert frontier and to tax and control nomadic pastoralists more easily. The military task was not an easy one, for there were both local revolts and attacks by indigenous people from beyond the frontier. In some areas even the farms had to be fortified.

So, how Roman was Roman North Africa? The immediate impression is that it was very Romanized. After all, one of the most famous of the Roman emperors, Septimius Severus, was born in Leptis Magna and apparently spoke Latin with a Punic accent. Many other people from North Africa also rose to prominence during the centuries of Roman rule: such as the soldier Lollius Urbicus, who became Governor of Britain; the writer Lucius Apuleius, whose book *The golden ass* is still read; and the early Christian leader St Augustine, who was to have such a great influence on the later Church. Other Africans, such as the client king Juba II, became highly acculturated, in his case founding the Roman city of Volubilis in western Morocco. Nevertheless, Roman North Africa remained a colony, in which a relatively small elite owing allegiance to Rome dominated the local people who were the bulk of the population. Punic, Berber and Libyan languages and cultures survived and in time many of the fine Roman cities were abandoned, as both the economic and political control of Rome weakened. After four centuries or so, the character of North Africa changed. Christianity became the official religion and the area under Roman control shrank. Although the colonial regime was to survive a Vandal invasion from Europe, it subsequently succumbed to Arab attack and the introduction of Islam. Significantly, the Romans, with their Mediterranean orientation, had rarely penetrated beyond the northern margin of the African continent but the Arabs understood deserts and they were to change all that.

16

QSAR ES-SEGHIR

Front door to Europe, front door to Africa

Some 1300 years ago North Africa was invaded by Arab people, and became an extension of the Islamic world of South-West Asia, as indigenous North Africans adopted its religion and culture. Nevertheless, North Africa also remained a part of the Mediterranean world, which included southern Europe. Indeed, the expansion of Islam into North Africa extended into Europe, controlling parts of what is now Spain and Portugal for almost 800 years. A succession of states and rulers came and went in different parts of the overall region and remarkable cultural developments took place, characterized by flourishing towns and cities, increasing trade and the pursuit of learning. In North Africa there were many centres of importance, such as Fez, Tangier, Algiers, Tunis, Kairouan and Tripoli but continuing occupation makes their archaeological investigation difficult. However, it has been possible to investigate thoroughly a small city that was abandoned over 450 years ago and never reoccupied. It was not an important city but for some centuries it played a significant role in the history of the western Mediterranean. The place had various names, of which the latest Arabic one was Qsar es-Seghir but the Portuguese knew it as Alcacer Ceguer. Located at the narrowest part of the Strait of Gibraltar, it was only 22 kilometres from the European shore. As a result it was, in succession, a conduit for people and commodities, a frontier fortress, and a colonial outpost. Occupied in turn by Moslem North Africans and then Christian Portuguese, its story is one of interaction between Africa and Europe.

Qsar es-Seghir existed at a time when we have documentary as well as archaeological evidence for this part of North Africa. The settlement seems to have originated about 1300 years ago, as an embarkation point for military forces crossing to the European shore. It continued in this role until about 700 years ago, when Islamic control of southern Spain approached its end. For the earlier part of this period there is little archaeological evidence at Qsar es-Seghir but during the later part the rulers of the area invested heavily in its fortification and development. However, its role changed with the loss of Spanish territory and for over a century it functioned as a trading port, although latterly suffering an economic decline probably caused by the Portuguese capture of the nearby port of Ceuta. Although of less importance

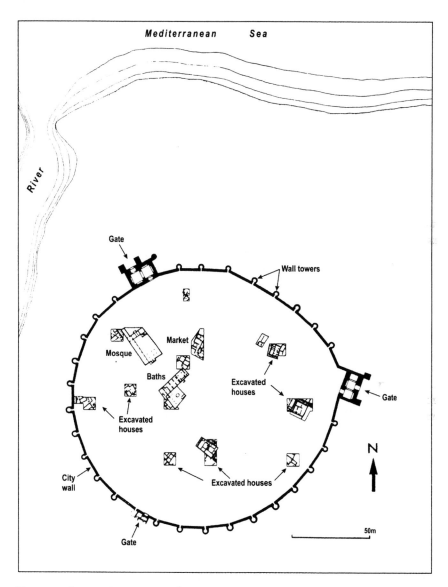

Labels within figure:

Mediterranean   Sea

River

Gate

Wall towers

Mosque

Market

Baths

Excavated houses

Excavated houses

Gate

Excavated houses

City wall

Gate

N

50m

Figure 37 Qsar es-Seghir, plan of the Islamic city as revealed by surviving structures and by excavation. Reproduced by permission of Elsevier from Redman, C.L. 1986. *Qsar es-Seghir: an archaeological view of medieval life.* Academic Press, London, Figure 3.2.

as an outlet for African goods than larger North African ports, the position of Qsar es-Seghir so close to the European coast must have given it an advantage. Furthermore, the commodities that it handled probably included some from beyond the Sahara, including West African gold for which there was such a demand in Europe.

Qsar es-Seghir was a planned city, its circular layout either by accident or intent conforming to an Islamic ideal supposedly represented by early Baghdad. Its relatively small area of less than 3 hectares was enclosed by a heavily mortared stone and fired-brick defensive wall, about 1.8 metres thick and 8 metres high. A total of 29 towers were located along this wall and access into the city was provided by three fortified gates. The city was situated in an area with a climate favourable to agriculture. It was close to the shore, to its north, and to a small river, to its west, that ran into the sea nearby. Within the city wall was a roughly rectangular layout of relatively wide streets, with the congregational mosque to the north-west, the public bath building near the centre, and the market to the north. These comprised the main public facilities. The mosque provided the centre-point for religious observance, the public bath was of religious and social importance as well as contributing to communal hygiene, and the market supplied foodstuffs and other necessities. All three had been carefully planned and were constructed in stone and fired brick, the one of which most survived when excavated being the bath build-ing. This was a most impressive structure, with a changing area, a cold room, a warm room, and a hot room, the floors of all being paved with bricks or tiles. Next to the hot room was a room containing a furnace, from which hot air cir-culated beneath the floor of the hot room. Adjacent to the building was a well to supply water. The whole complex is a reminder of how much Islamic society had inherited from the preceding Roman world.

Much of the remaining space within the city wall was filled with houses of stone and fired brick, a small number also being outside the wall. The houses were rectangular in plan, with windowless exteriors and a single entrance from the street through a bent-axis corridor. Within each house, the rooms were ranged around a central court and included living/sleeping rooms, a kitchen, a storage space and a latrine. The latter emptied into an underground drain, that fed into a drainage system running under the middle of the adjacent street and then possibly into several soakaways. Each house also had a well but usually lacked a hearth because cooking appears to have been done on pottery braziers containing charcoal. The main food eaten was bread and couscous (both made from wheat) and beef and mutton. Floors could be of earth but were often plastered (and sometimes painted) or paved with bricks or tiles. Walls were plastered, and towards the end of the Islamic period more decorative coloured tiling was used on floors. Although many houses were of only one storey, some had a second storey reached by an internal stairway. The overall emphasis in house design was on privacy from the rest of the community and simple comfort within each house.

Figure 38 The public bath building in the Islamic city of Qsar es-Seghir, as excavated. View from changing area end. Reproduced by permission of Elsevier from Redman, C.L. 1986. *Qsar es-Seghir: an archaeological view of
medieval life.* Academic Press, London, Figure 3.15.

Simplicity is also reflected by the pottery and other objects that were excavated from the houses. Most of the pottery was wheel-made but undecorated, sometimes with a clear lead glaze on the interior in order to hold liquids more efficiently. Much of it was probably made in the city or in the surrounding district but there were also more decorative ceramics that were mostly brought from elsewhere in North Africa and from Islamic Spain. Iron was used for weapons, tools and nails but does not seem to have been plentiful. Items of personal adornment were made of bronze or brass, sometimes coated in silver or gold. Bone and ivory were made use of and glass vessels were in use but very rarely. Islamic coins of gold, silver and copper were also found but very few of them. The general impression from both the houses and the objects found within them was that some people were wealthier than others but not to any great extent. Partly this might be because of Islamic restraint in display but more likely it is because Qsar es-Seghir was a small city of workers and traders, whose population never grew beyond 1200–1300 inhabitants.

Islamic Qasr es-Seghir came to a violent end 550 years ago when it was attacked by a Portuguese army equipped with cannon, against which its walls were no protection. Its inhabitants surrendered and were allowed to leave, taking their possessions with them. Renamed Alcacer Ceguer, the city became part of a Portuguese expansion into north-west Africa, that eventually included Tangier and several ports along the Atlantic coast. As such it was a fortress city, with modernized fortifications, a garrison of soldiers and a population that was predominantly male. With the passage of time, it gradually became a military colony, with some civilian inhabitants and growing economic activity, but it never had full control of the surrounding region. Eventually, expenditure on the defence of its North African possessions and the relative profitability of its other more distant overseas interests led Portugal to abandon North Africa altogether. After only 92 years the Portuguese left Qsar es-Seghir, first destroying many of its buildings and some of its fortifications to discourage reuse of the site. In this, at least, they were successful and the place was never reoccupied.

The Portuguese city was very different from the preceding Islamic one. Although it retained the circular plan, its defensive walls were reduced in height and broadened at the base, as well as being surrounded by a deep ditch. Five bastions were also built, three of them around the former city gates. The one closest to the sea became a fortified citadel, from which a covered passageway extended 110 metres to the shore, providing protection for landing supplies. All of these modifications were designed to make the city more easily defended against cannon fire and to enable the efficient use of cannons and firearms against attackers. Indeed, two sieges of the city by Islamic forces were unsuccessful. Within the city, the street layout seems to have remained much as it had been previously but with a greater number of open spaces at the ends or intersections of streets, most of which were paved with cobbles. As for public facilities, the mosque was turned into a church on the very day that the Portuguese occupied the city and was subsequently

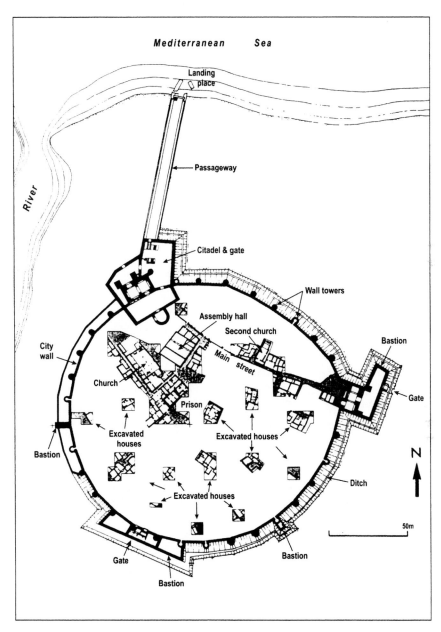

Figure 39 Qsar es-Seghir, plan of the Portuguese city as revealed by surviving struc-
tures and by excavation. Reproduced by permission of Elsevier from
Redman, C.L. 1986. *Qsar es-Seghir: an archaeological view of medieval life.*
Academic Press, London, Figure 5.2.

rebuilt. A second church was also built, as well as a large building that seems to have served as an assembly hall. The old market disappeared and the public bath building was turned into a prison or arsenal. For the Portuguese its religious and social functions were irrelevant and apparently they had less interest in personal cleanliness than their Islamic predecessors.

The houses in the Portuguese city also differed from the Islamic ones, although in many cases the earlier buildings were reused. Their plan was usually linear, with rooms that were increasingly private as one moved away from the largest one, to which an often decorative front door gave access. Many houses were also the location of commercial activities and were not as well finished internally as the Moslem houses had been. Although still built mainly of stone, they lacked the latrines and drains of the earlier houses, chamber pots presumably being used instead. In addition, fewer houses had their own wells, public wells in the city also being in use. Furthermore, household cooking seems to have been done on hearths, not on charcoal braziers as previously. The main food was similar to that of the Islamic period but pork and beef were the most common meat, significant amounts of fish and shellfish were also eaten, and wine was drunk. Many houses were subdivided as time went on, probably because of a growing population, which might have reached about 1000 people. There were also signs of differences in wealth, although the pottery and other objects excavated from the houses were more informative on this matter.

The Portuguese occupants of Qsar es-Seghir seem to have had more personal possessions than their predecessors and to have been more interested in items of display. Most of the pottery was no longer of local origin but was imported from across the Strait of Gibraltar. Much of this was glazed tableware, and included decorated pieces that came from Portugal, Spain, Italy and Germany. Latterly there was even some Chinese porcelain. In addition, there was a variety of metal objects, including weapons, armour and tools, mainly of iron, as well as numerous items of personal adornment, of bronze, silver and gold. Glass vessels and bracelets were also common and coins were much more numerous than they had been during the Islamic period, although most were copper ones, with only a few of silver. Collectively, the evidence suggested a three-tier hierarchy, consisting of a large number of people of relatively modest means, a small number who were rather wealthier, and just one who was richer than anyone else; reflecting a typical military community into which civilians were gradually included as appropriate.

Qsar es-Seghir was only a small city and must have been overshadowed by the many larger centres in Islamic North Africa. Nevertheless, its story can to some extent represent their stories. In addition, its unique position at the narrowest part of the Strait of Gibraltar has provided an eloquent archaeological record of the interaction of two cultures, Islamic African and Christian European. Basically this was because it was a front door, for Africans one that gave access to Europe, for Europeans one that gave access to Africa. When it ceased to be relevant in that role, it ceased to exist.

17

JENNÉ-JENO

An early city on the Middle Niger

For the last few thousand years the Sahara Desert has made contact difficult between Mediterranean North Africa and West Africa. Difficult but not impossible. The existence of important resources south of the desert, particularly gold, stimulated extensive trade across the desert, using camel transport, from a little more than 1000 years ago. The development of this trade was only possible because there were already communities in West Africa who were able to handle the procurement, transport and exchange of commodities from the West African interior and the distribution of merchandise from the Sahara and the Mediterranean world that was offered in exchange. Some of the most important of these communities were those situated where the savanna and the desert meet. This is because they were in the front line of contact with traders from the north, whose activities they could to some extent control and benefit from. This was particularly the case along the Middle Niger, where that river swings north in a great bend that brings it to the very edge of the desert but provides an environment capable of supporting a substantial human population, although one that has varied as climatic conditions have fluctuated. Many towns and cities were to grow up along this part of the Niger during the last 1000 years or so, some of them becoming famous such as Timbuktu and Gao. During a similar period a succession of states were also to rise and fall: Ghana, Mali and Songhai being the principal ones. As is now realized, however, the origins of these developments were over 1000 years earlier. Some of the most important evidence for this comes from the site of Jenné-jeno, near the present city of Jenné.

Jenné-jeno is situated in a part of the Middle Niger region that is often called the Inland Niger Delta. About 10,000 years ago the river did not flow to the Atlantic Ocean as it does now but drained north into lakes and marshes in what is now the desert, in the process building up a delta of river sediments. This has since become a relatively fertile area of river channels and lakes that is subject to large-scale seasonal flooding. Although the climate in this southern part of the modern state of Mali is both hot and dry, with only a short wet season, immense quantities of water from the higher

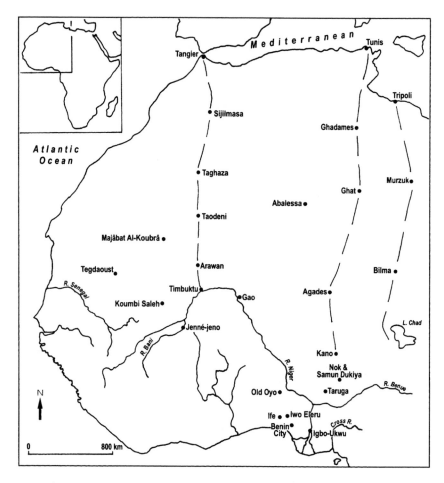

Figure 40 Important sites and places in West and North-West Africa. Refer to Chapters 17–21. Map by Sue Singleton.

rainfall area of the Upper Niger flow down the river each year, bringing fertile silt. As a result, the Middle Niger has long been attractive to human settlement, providing important resources of fish from both the river and its floodwaters and enabling the growing of West African rice in the areas that flood and of native millet on the higher sandy ground. In addition, large numbers of cattle, goats and sheep can be raised by exploiting the various local environments at different seasons; grazing the desert margins after the brief rains and feeding on the vegetation and crop residues of the river channels and basins during the dry season.

Nevertheless, life for the farmers, herdsmen and fishermen of the Middle Niger has often been unpredictable: the floodwaters brought by the river each year might be either too little for their purposes or so great that they swept away houses and drowned people and animals. Or the floodwaters might arrive too early or too late or not arrive at all. In addition, as the centuries passed, there were gradual changes in the climate of this part of West Africa, so that at times it was highly productive and supported a dense population but at others it was afflicted by drought and famine, and the number of inhabitants declined. The unpredictability of this environment created both opportunities and constraints, which were complicated by the variety of landforms within short distances of each other. The various groups of Mande people, who have occupied the area for the last few thousand years, developed a series of highly flexible responses to this situation. Different varieties of rice were grown in different depths of water, the type of millets and other food crops planted were chosen to suit the varied conditions, herdsmen learnt the best time to seek grazing in each area and adjusted their movements to suit the season, fishermen evolved a variety of strategies for catching different species at different times. In short, the unpredictability of the Middle Niger encouraged a remarkable level of human adaptability.

It is this adaptability that has allowed the concentration of population along the Middle Niger for the last 2000 years or more. Compared with the desert to its north or the savanna to its south, this has been an agriculturally productive area that in good times had surplus food to trade with its less fortunate neighbours. However, its river channels, basins and lakes, and its sand ridges and dunes, lacked some of the resources that its people needed, such as iron ore from which to smelt iron for tools and weapons, salt, and many other commodities. These had to be obtained from outside the region, so there grew up a trading network that reached far into the surrounding areas. It was by means of this network that North African and Saharan traders were eventually able to tap the gold, ivory, kola, slaves and other things that they sought from the West African interior. It was also through this network of trading contacts that the salt, manufactured goods and other commodities from the Sahara and the Mediterranean world were distributed. The Middle Niger region thus came to play a major role in long-distance trade; camel caravans terminated at its more important cities and towns, boats moved both local and foreign goods along its maze of waterways, donkeys or human porters provided transport to and from the savanna and forests to its south. For outsiders from the north, this area constituted the limits of their knowledge. To it they brought new ideas as well as trade goods, of which the most important was the Islamic religion.

It was Islam that brought writing to the area, so that we know something about developments over the last 1000 years or so; European writers only providing information for the last few centuries. Our knowledge of the Middle Niger before the earliest written accounts has to be obtained from the remains of the places where people lived and of the things that they made and used or obtained by trade. Mounds of debris, many relatively small, some large, a few very large, consist of the remnants of their mud-built houses and the accumulated waste of everyday life, such as broken pottery, discarded meat bones and other food scraps, ash and charcoal from cooking fires, and so on. In addition there are many burials of the people themselves, often in or near the settlements. From all this evidence it is pos-sible to reconstruct how people lived and something of their history. It is to this task that Jenné-jeno has made such an important contribution.

It seems that before about 3000 years ago the part of the Middle Niger in which Jenné-jeno is situated was so often covered by river floodwater that it was not regularly occupied, although there must have been hunters, plant-food gatherers, and fishermen in the vicinity. Farmers and herdsmen might also have been nearby because there is evidence of them at Jenné-jeno from about 2500 years ago. By that time its inhabitants were already growing rice and keeping cattle, as well as raising other crops, and fishing and collecting wild plant food. In addition, they were smelting iron from iron ore brought from outside the area. They built houses of sticks and mud and made fine pottery. By about 2000 years ago their village had grown into a small town and by about 1000 years ago it had become a city of perhaps as many as 13,000 people, protected by a city wall 2 kilometres long. Agriculture remained unchanged but trade had increased, pottery was more varied, the houses were now solidly built of mud brick, and pavements were made of potsherds. Fired clay figurines of animals and humans were also produced, probably for ritual use, some of them displaying remarkable artistic skill. There is little indication, however, that some people were richer or more important than others and it seems unlikely that the city was governed by any one individual. Most probably authority was vested in the older men, particularly those who had distinguished themselves in their trade or profes-sion or who had special sacred knowledge. They must have gained enough power to be able to persuade their fellow citizens to construct the protective city wall.

This raises interesting questions about the growth of urbanism in other places, both in Africa and elsewhere. At Jenné-jeno, apart from the city wall, there is no sign of the monumental architecture that has often been thought

Figure 41 Excavation through the settlement mound formed by the remains of the city of Jenné-jeno, Mali. Reproduced by permission of Rod McIntosh.

to indicate the presence of a ruling elite, or of the rich burials frequently provided for the privileged. Probably these were later aspects of urban development, unlike conditions at Jenné-jeno which indicate an earlier stage. Consequently it has been suggested that Jenné-jeno is unlikely to have controlled its surrounding area in the manner of the later savanna states. Nevertheless, it does seem to have formed the centre of a concentration of lesser settlements, of which no less than twenty-five lay within a 1-kilometre radius, making an urban cluster with a total population perhaps as high as 50,000 people. There was also a similarity of material culture over a large part of the Middle Niger and it is possible that at the peak of its growth Jenné-jeno might indeed have been the most important settlement in an area that had common economic, social and perhaps political interests.

The problem with the archaeological investigation of early urbanism and its development is that the main sites are often so extensive and, if they have been occupied for many centuries, have such deep deposits that excavation can only examine a very small part of each one of them. This is as true of Jenné-jeno as of many such sites but it is from such a small sample of the evidence that generalizations about the character of the city have to be made. Furthermore, in order to understand the relationship of such a city to its surrounding area and the lesser settlements in it, extensive regional survey is also necessary. In the case of Jenné-jeno, every effort has been made to ensure as representative a selection of evidence as possible. There has even been a systematic programme of drilling cores from the deposits at Jenné-jeno itself and at the nearby city of Jenné. This has enabled the sampling of far larger areas than would have been possible with conventional excavation alone.

Jenné-jeno and the sites in its vicinity are representative rather than unique. That is to say that the Inland Niger Delta contains many other sites of a similar age, some of which are also large, but they have only recently begun to be investigated. However, it does appear that Jenné-jeno played a particularly important role in the region. Not only was it able to tap the trade commodities of the West African interior to its south and west but the Niger River and its tributary the Bani River enabled it to market its surplus food in less fortunate areas downstream, such as that of Timbuktu. In addition it was well placed to profit from the development of trans-Saharan trade from late in the first millennium AD onwards. Although climatic deterioration led to a decline in the population of the Middle Niger after about 1000 years ago, the area nevertheless made an important contribution to the world economy during the first half of the second millennium AD, handling much of the gold that reached Europe at that time. Jenné-jeno has not only thrown new light on the indigenous origins of urbanism in the West African savanna, it has also demonstrated the significance of the Middle Niger in the history of Africa as a whole.

18

VOYAGES IN THE SAHARA

The desert trade with West Africa

In recent millennia the Sahara Desert has been one of the world's most formidable barriers to human contact. Until about 1300 years ago it effectively formed the southern edge of the world known to Europe and the Mediterranean. Together with the navigational dangers of its Atlantic coast, the desert prevented or at least severely limited contact between that world and the West African savannas and forests. This situation changed with the arrival in North Africa of Arab people, many of whom came from a desert background and understood the value of the camel, an animal that had already been introduced into North Africa. Sustained by their Islamic faith and powerful commercial incentives, they and the indigenous Berber people developed a network of trade routes across the Sahara. They found that south of the desert there were commodities much in demand to its north, particularly gold and slaves, and that manufactures from the north and salt from the desert itself were amongst goods equally sought after in the south. The long-distance trade that developed, often despite great difficulties and dangers, persisted for over a thousand years, only declining with the development of European maritime trade along the West African coast in recent centuries. By then it had brought about major cultural changes in much of West Africa.

It is possible that there was contact across the Sahara before the advent of the Arabs and their camels. As early as about 2500 years ago it was recorded that the inhabitants of the Fezzan area in the northern Sahara had horse-drawn chariots, in which they chased other people. Furthermore, rock engravings representing both horse-drawn and ox-drawn vehicles have been found along two main axes across the desert, stretching from North Africa to the Niger. It has been argued that this indicates the existence of pre-Roman trade routes to West Africa but this seems unlikely. It is significant, for instance, that although Roman material, including coins, has been found far beyond some of the other imperial frontiers, none of it seems to have reached the southern side of the Sahara. The most southerly Roman evidence comes from an elite female burial at Abalessa, in the Hoggar area of the central desert. This and the fact that trade goods from the Sahara did reach

Figure 42 A loaded pack-camel. From Junker, W. 1890. *Travels in Africa during the years 1875–1878.* Chapman and Hall, London, Page 8.

some of the Roman cities of North Africa (Chapter 15) would suggest that there were exchange networks within and around the desert but that they operated in relatively limited areas rather than reaching from one side of the Sahara to the other. Thus commodities could have arrived in North Africa from great distances away but only after changing hands many times in a long chain of transactions. Wheeled vehicles might have been used in some areas but pack animals such as bullocks or donkeys are also a possibility, particularly if conditions in the desert were slightly less harsh than they are known to have been later. Both of these animals have a greater ability to go without water than is often thought.

However, camels are the pack animals best adapted to hot and dry conditions. Often carrying more than 300 kilograms each, they can cover 20–25 kilometres a day for extended periods. They can voluntarily go without water for up to 10 days and for much longer if browsing on plants with a high water content. When water does become available they can drink up to 180 litres within 24 hours and absorb it quickly. They can eat thorny plants that other animals avoid and have huge soft feet specially adapted to walking on soft sand. Camels bred for riding can cover up to 13 kilometres per hour at their usual pace and average 65–80 kilometres a day for up to 2 weeks. Without doubt, it was the widespread use of camels that opened up the trade routes across the Sahara. Yet it was also the skill of their handlers that brought this about. The single-humped camel that was used in North

Africa is thought to have been domesticated in the deserts of southern Arabia and it was desert Arabs from that general area who first learnt how to overcome the problems of saddling and how to breed and manage these animals. A late introduction to Roman North Africa, camels were mainly used to pull ploughs and carts until the arrival of Arab people who understood their real value for carrying loads or riders in arid conditions. It was such people who first called the camel 'the ship of the desert' and it was this animal that made possible the voyages in the Sahara on which they, and the Islamized peoples of the desert and its northern margins, now embarked.

Like voyages at sea, these journeys of camel caravans had very real dangers. Wells were few and some of the longer stages in between them could only be completed by sending a messenger ahead to the next well, to get water sent out to meet the caravan. Dust storms could impede progress and fill the wells with sand. Attacks by desert nomads were a constant threat, in spite of payments for safe passage and the frequent employment of such people in the caravans. Sickness and injury to both humans and camels, on journeys that could last several months, were added to the risk of starvation or dehydration. Furthermore, parts of some routes were not easy to follow and there was a serious danger of a caravan getting lost. Little wonder that writers recorded desiccated human bodies left lying by the track and commented on the large number of camel skeletons along some routes. Only 200 years ago a caravan of 2000 men and 1800 camels, heading north from Timbuktu, died of thirst, every man and every animal. Archaeology has produced evidence of the problems that could arise. In the lonely Majâbat Al-Koubrâ, halfway across the desert, the abandoned loads of a caravan were found to have been buried in a sand dune over 800 years ago. Consisting of brass rods and cowrie shells, they had clearly belonged to a caravan heading south that had run into trouble and attempted to save itself by reducing its loads. The fact that they had not been subsequently recovered suggests that even this desperate measure was unsuccessful.

It was sheer profit that drove men to take such risks: the gains from the Saharan trade could be enormous. Commodities purchased south of the desert might sell for five times as much when they reached the North African coast. The problem was getting them there and over the centuries a whole network of routes was used to accomplish this. Excluding lesser routes, there were three ways to get to West Africa, each of which took about two months. First, and best known, was the western route, running from southern Morocco to the middle Niger River. Its course varied over time, but seems to have been often Sijilmasa, in the north, through Taghaza, Taodeni and Arawan, to Timbuktu in the south. It was this route that was most important for tapping the gold of West Africa, whose sources in the headwaters of the Niger and Senegal Rivers were kept secret by the West African merchants who sold it. Much of this gold eventually reached Europe, enabling some countries to introduce gold currency about 700 years

Figure 43 Gold disc from Rao, Senegal, diameter 184 millimetres, weight 191 grams. From Joire, J. 1943. Archaeological discoveries in Senegal. *Man* 43, Page 49 (Blackwell Publishing, Oxford).

ago. Other commodities that travelled north along the western route included slaves, ivory, ebony, wild animal skins, peppers and civet (a secretion from civet cats used in perfume). Coming south the most important commodity was salt, particularly from the central desert mines at Taghaza and Taodeni, but European manufactured goods, especially cloth, and copper were also important, as were sugar, brass vessels, dates and horses from Morocco and elsewhere in North Africa. Archaeological evidence from southern towns such as Koumbi Saleh, Tegdaoust and Gao confirm the scale of this trade, marble gravestones at the latter place, for instance, being brought all the way from Spain some 900 years ago.

The second of the main trade routes was the central one leading from modern Tunisia through Ghadames, Ghat and Agades to Hausaland, in what is now northern Nigeria. At the southern end of this route was Kano, which in recent centuries became one of the most important commercial centres in the West African savanna. Going north along this route was a variety of goods amongst which slaves were more important than gold and other commodities included fine leatherwork, dyed cloth and kola nuts. Coming south were European manufactured products, coarse silk from Tripoli, copper and horses. There was also a huge amount of salt, mainly from Bilma in the southern Sahara to the north-east of Kano. This was carried by a special annual caravan that as recently as 100 years ago, when it was already in decline, still consisted of no less than 20,000 camels. So important was the trade of Hausaland that Hausa became the market language for much of the West African savanna.

The third route was the eastern one, from Tripoli, through Murzuk and Bilma, to Borno in the Lake Chad area. The principal commodity travelling south was salt from Bilma but manufactured goods and copper were also important and there was a particular demand in the south for horses and, in more recent centuries, for guns. In exchange there was a variety of exports including ivory, animal skins, gold and other things but by far the most important on this route were slaves. Borno sent out regular slaving expeditions to its south, in order to supply an almost insatiable North African market. Young men and women were particularly sought after, but it was castrated males for which the slave trade on the eastern route was best known. Boys and youths subjected to such mutilation had only a 10 per cent chance of survival and the long march across the desert exacted a heavy toll on all slaves. In later times the route was said to be strewn with human skeletons and even those slaves who survived the journey had to be rested and fattened near its northern end before they were marketable.

The development of trans-Saharan trade had consequences for both North Africa and West Africa. To the former it brought wealth, in the form of gold, slaves, ivory and other valued commodities, but it also brought knowledge of a previously unknown part of the world. For the latter, it not only provided manufactured products from the north and salt from the desert but also had a profound cultural impact particularly on societies in the savanna. Urbanism, state formation and trading networks in West Africa had origins that predated the camel caravans (Chapter 17) but it was nevertheless the profits from the Saharan trade that stimulated the further growth of all three. In addition, repeated contacts with Islamic people from beyond and within the desert led to the introduction of the Islamic faith, together with much of its associated culture. With the caravans were visiting merchants, travellers, scholars and holy men, and with them came books and literacy in Arabic. However, the desert routes had detrimental as well as beneficial effects in the south. They permitted the growth of an international slave trade that destabilized parts of West Africa. They also enabled a Moroccan army of 5600 men, 8000 camels and 1000 pack-horses to invade the Middle Niger some 400 years ago, with disastrous consequences.

The caravans of the old Sahara are gone, their trade almost completely wiped out in recent centuries by European maritime activity along the West African coast. A trading network oriented towards the desert was replaced by one oriented towards the Atlantic Ocean. The abolition of slavery, the near exhaustion of gold and ivory resources, and the construction of roads and railways, also contributed to this fundamental change in economic organization. Nevertheless, for over 1000 years the trans-Saharan trade had brought West Africa into contact with the rest of the world. This was no mean achievement for the humble camels and the men who accompanied them.

19

IGBO-UKWU

A challenge from the past

Almost seventy years ago a man was digging a cistern near his house in the town of Igbo-Ukwu in eastern Nigeria. Although the area had abundant rainfall, water supply could be a problem during the annual dry season and so underground storage that filled during the wet season was frequently resorted to. He had got to a depth of about half a metre when he began to dig out bronze objects that looked very old. An official of the then British colonial government heard about this discovery and purchased the items. He published an account of the Igbo-Ukwu finds and subsequently presented them to Nigeria's principal museum but there the matter rested for over twenty years. Only then were archaeological excavations carried out at this place, where it appeared that discoveries had been made at various times in three different locations. The technical and artistic quality of the artefacts that had been given to the museum was so high, and so little was then known of the human history of the area from which they had come, that it was obviously important to ascertain who had made them and when. The general assumption was that they had been made by the Igbo people who live in this part of Nigeria but were not very old. However, the results of the excavations were to astonish everyone and even cause some to doubt their findings. Now, many years later, the Igbo-Ukwu evidence still raises questions and continues to be a challenge from the past, requiring that we re-examine long-held ideas.

For a long time many outsiders misunderstood the West African rainforest, regarding it as a difficult environment that was unlikely to have been the location of important cultural developments in the past. This was in spite of obvious evidence to the contrary, such as at Benin City (Chapter 21) and other places. It was also in spite of accounts by some of the European visitors over the last 500 years or so. Nevertheless, the conviction remained that much of the rainforest consisted of dense natural vegetation that was unaffected by human settlement and which had few resources to offer. Nothing could be further from the truth and it is now realized that most of the forest has been subject to shifting agricultural exploitation at one time or another, and in some areas many times over. Indeed some parts of it, particularly on its edges, have been permanently altered by many centuries of farming, especially for the cultivation of yams and the growing of oil palms, which together have formed the basis of food supplies. Also, although tsetse flies have discouraged the keeping of domestic livestock, the presence of small numbers of trypanosomiasis-resistant dwarf goats and cattle indicate that they have nevertheless been kept for a long time. In addition, the forest and its margins have provided a range of other resources. The outcome has been remarkable human population growth in some areas, particularly east of the Niger River in what is now eastern Nigeria. This was the setting of the Igbo-Ukwu discoveries, which offered a fresh insight into the past achievements of people in the area.

All three excavation sites were within 100 metres of each other, in an area of Igbo-Ukwu covered by houses and compounds, making excavation particularly difficult. This meant that it was impossible to examine the stratigraphic relationship of the sites to one another or to their more general archaeological context. Nevertheless, the highly distinctive cultural material that was recovered from the three sites was so similar that they appeared to be closely related. First, there was the site where the cistern digger had made his discoveries. Although the deposit had been disturbed, it was possible to see that it had consisted of a collection of bronze, copper and iron objects, together with pots and over 63,000 glass and stone beads, all of which had been laid out carefully at about the same level in a rectangular area of 2–3 by 3–4 metres, approximately 60–70 centimetres below the surface. The metal artefacts included a spectacular bronze pot on its own stand and enclosed in a cage of bronze knotted rope-work, the whole just over 32 centimetres in height. This was highly decorated, as were most of the other bronze items present, which included bowls shaped like calabashes, an openwork stand, ornaments for staffs, a belt made up of separate pieces, imitations of large marine shells, small representations of animal and human heads, and various other things. All of this material had been manufactured by means of the lost-wax casting process. This is a method that involves modelling the object in wax and then covering it with clay, in which a hole is left to pour out the molten wax from the heated mould and then pour in the molten metal. In principle the method is simple but in execution it can be very complex and require a high level of skill. It was immediately apparent that the craftsmen who had made the Igbo-Ukwu bronzes had been technically brilliant, as well as having a quite unique art style. This impression was reinforced by the other artefacts present, items of copper or iron that indicated smithing skills, and pots with decoration in high relief that were outstanding examples of the potter's craft. Fragments of cloth amongst the artefacts suggested the manufacture of textiles as well, although the materials might have resulted from long-distance trade, as was assumed to be the case with the numerous beads.

The second site was very different. Again there was a remarkable collection

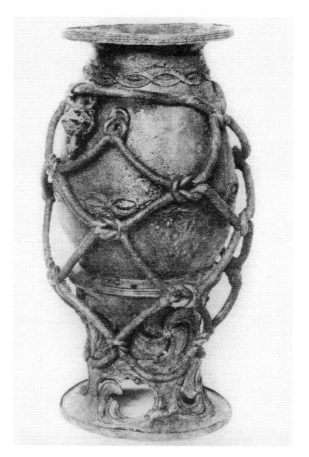

Figure 44 Bronze pot and stand, enclosed in bronze knotted rope-work, height just
over 32 centimetres. From Igbo-Ukwu, eastern Nigeria. Reproduced by
permission of Thurstan Shaw from Shaw, T. 1977. *Unearthing Igbo-Ukwu:
archaeological discoveries in eastern Nigeria.* Oxford University Press, Ibadan,
Figure 3.1.

of artefacts but the lowest of them lay at a depth of almost 3.5 metres and
their arrangement seemed in part to have resulted from some sort of collapse, rather than from deliberate placement. The objects also differed somewhat from those of the first site. There were three large elephant tusks and
most of the metal items were of smithed copper rather than cast bronze,
including a crown, a fan-holder, a plate to be worn on the chest, two circles
of spiral bosses set in wood which appeared to be the remains of a stool,
numerous anklets, beaded armlets, and other things. There were only two
items of cast bronze but both were important, one consisting of a hilt
depicting a man mounted on a horse or donkey, and the other in the shape

114

Figure 45 Bronze openwork altar-stand, height 27.5 centimetres. From Igbo-Ukwu, eastern Nigeria. Reproduced by permission of Thurstan Shaw from Shaw, T. 1977. *Unearthing Igbo-Ukwu: archaeological discoveries in eastern Nigeria.* Oxford University Press, Ibadan, Figure 3.37.

of a leopard's skull mounted on a copper rod. In addition, the excavation recovered over 102,000 glass and stone beads, and amongst the artefacts were badly decayed human bones, including most of a skull, indicating the burial of a single individual. A number of pieces of iron were also recovered and at a level higher in the excavation were found human remains from at least five more individuals.

The third of the Igbo-Ukwu sites was different again. It consisted of an infilled pit almost 3 metres deep, of which the top had been destroyed by modern disturbance. It appeared to have been dug specially to receive its filling, which consisted of layers of reddish sandy soil alternating with dark grey burnt material. There was also a lot of bone but in such poor condition that very few fragments could be identified, the majority of those being of antelope and duiker. Amongst the metal artefacts were two staff ornaments of cast bronze and a number of copper or bronze wristlets. There were also several items of iron. However, it was pottery that was most common in this pit, including some complete pots. These were similar in style to pottery from the other sites but included one really remarkable vessel over 40 centimetres in height. This was heavily decorated in high relief with ridges, grooving and bosses and with two skilfully modelled coiled snakes, a chameleon, a ram's head, and an unidentifiable object that looked like a mat. Finally, at this site there was a virtual absence of beads, contrasting with the other two sites which had produced such large numbers.

So what did it all mean? First of all, what were the activities that had produced these three different sets of evidence that nevertheless seemed closely related? The second site was the easiest to understand: it apparently represented the burial of an important individual who had been seated on a stool, wearing and accompanied by ceremonial regalia. The burial had been within a wooden chamber on the top of which at least five more burials, perhaps sacrifices, were placed, the hole containing the chamber then being filled in. In time, the chamber had collapsed, leaving its contents in the disarray in which they were found. The first site was more difficult to understand but seemed likely to have been a shrine in which ceremonial regalia was kept, perhaps consisting of a small open-fronted building. Why it had collapsed with its contents intact is unknown but may have been because of the power of its sacred objects, that people feared to remove. Lastly, the third site was clearly a pit that had been dug in order to dispose of ritual material, that for some reason could no longer be used or had lost its relevance. Collectively, it was thought that the sites were associated with the former existence of a 'priest king' similar to the Eze Nri, a position that survived to modern times as the highest politico-ritual title in some Igbo areas.

All of this was remarkable enough but it was the date that really started the arguments. Charcoal and wood from the excavations were submitted for radiocarbon dating but the samples from the first site were destroyed due to the failure of laboratory equipment and only the second and third sites could be dated. The results indicated an age of a little over 1000 years, much earlier than some people had expected. The main problem was the sophistication of the casting technology, some of the bronzes being so complex in their design and ornamentation that their production must have required a very high level of skill. How or from where had such skill been acquired at such an early date? There was also the matter of the approximately 165,000 glass and stone beads. No evidence existed for ancient glass manufacture in the area and many of the stone beads were of carnelian that was not available locally. They must, therefore, be evidence of long-distance trade, and its development at such an early date was questioned. In addition, at the time of the excavations it was thought that Nigeria lacked sources of copper and that this must also have come from far away, although it has now been found that copper, tin and lead (the main constituents of the Igbo-Ukwu bronzes) could all have been obtained locally.

As time went on, the Igbo-Ukwu dates were generally accepted as correct but the problem remained of explaining such an accumulation of wealth as was represented by the Igbo-Ukwu evidence. The beads at least had a remote source, Egypt via routes across the Sahara or skirting its southern edge seemed the most likely, but what had the people of Igbo-Ukwu given in exchange? Ivory was suggested as the most likely commodity but this would have been available to Saharan and savanna traders without going so far to the south. Silver was another suggestion, present in small quantities in local lead deposits, but did the sophisticated technology exist to extract it? Overlooked, perhaps, was the probably high agricultural productivity of the Igbo-Ukwu region and its access to the major trade routes of the Niger and Benue rivers. The beads, like the horse or donkey depicted in one of the bronzes, could have been part of many localized transactions before they ended up in the rainforest, perhaps in exchange for yams, a food that is easily transported. Significantly, the third site, possibly the earliest of the three, had virtually no beads, suggesting that important developments had already occurred locally before such exotic items began to penetrate the area.

Such is the Igbo-Ukwu story, a story of which the end has still to be written. The evidence from these three related sites has challenged archaeologists and historians to re-examine their ideas about the past of the West African rainforest and has raised questions for some of which answers are still being sought.

20

ANCESTRAL FACES

Ancient sculpture in Nigeria

From the upper parts of the Niger River to those of the Congo River, there is a huge area of tropical Africa in which some of the most powerful evidence from the past consists of art in the form of sculpture. Most common amongst this material are wood carvings, of which for climatic reasons the surviving examples are only a century or two old, but fortunately in some areas there are also items of fired clay, of metal, and of stone that have survived much longer. This is particularly the case in the modern state of Nigeria, where there is a remarkable amount and variety of sculptured art, some of which is over 2000 years old. Two of the most important later examples of this are from Igbo-Ukwu (Chapter 19) and Benin City (Chapter 21) but there are many others. Much of this material is representational, depicting animals or human beings, in the latter case literally providing us with faces from the past. Some of these seem to have been of deities but others were probably of rulers and other people in the societies that produced the sculptures. Consequently, these works of art are a potential source of information on religious, political, social, economic and technological matters, as well as on artistic style and the way people saw their world. However, to realize that potential it is necessary to investigate also the archaeological context of the art and sometimes this has not had enough attention.

For a long time this was the problem with the terracotta (fired clay) sculptures that were named after the village of Nok, in central Nigeria, where they were first found. Examples of this art style were discovered accidentally during the mining of alluvial tin, their often deep stratigraphic locations being the result of natural erosion and deposition. In other words, they were not in their original positions and this made it difficult to date them or to know whether other evidence found with them really belonged with them. However, the Nok material was clearly an extremely important body of art, with distinctive stylistic characteristics, and it has become justifiably famous. Most remarkable was the fine modelling of a number of life-sized and near life-sized human heads, that had apparently formed parts of complete figures of which fragments were also found. The facial features

118

Figure 46 Terracotta head in the Nok style, from Jemaa, central Nigeria. Height nearly 23 centimetres. From Fagg, B. The Nok Culture. *West African Review* December 1956, Page 30.

were sharply delineated, suggesting inspiration from now-vanished wood carvings, often with triangular eyes whose pupils were represented by holes into the hollow interior of the terracotta. Many of the items also showed details of hair, beards, dress, headgear, personal adornment, even diseased conditions. In addition to the human representations, there were also other subjects, including monkeys, elephants, snakes, a tick, and fluted pumpkins. As time went on, examples of this distinctive Nok art style were found across a wide area, about 500 kilometres long and 150 kilometres wide, stretching from west of the Jos Plateau to south of the Benue River. Nevertheless, the age of this material remained uncertain and its relevance ambiguous.

Eventually two sites were found and excavated where the archaeological evidence was in its original location. Radiocarbon dating indicated that both belonged to the period between about 2500 and 2000 years ago, making the

Nok sculptures some of the oldest in tropical Africa. One of these sites was at Samun Dukiya in the Nok valley and was clearly an occupation site. It produced broken pottery, iron and other artefacts and fragments of terracottas in the Nok style. The other site was at Taruga, almost 100 kilometres to the south-west of Nok, and appeared to have been principally an industrial site. The remains of a number of iron-smelting furnaces were excavated, amongst the oldest that have been found in tropical Africa (Chapter 9). There were also broken pottery, iron and other artefacts and again fragments of Nok-style terracottas. From these two sites it is apparent that the makers of the Nok terracottas were iron-using farmers and it has been suggested that the artwork was made for use on shrines concerned with the fertility of the land. The erosion and deposition, that created the deep alluvial deposits in which most of the terracottas were found, is thought to have occurred between about 3500 years ago and about 1800 years ago, and possibly resulted largely from agricultural clearance and tree-cutting to provide fuel for iron-smelting. However, the significance of the Nok terracottas still remains imperfectly understood. Stylistic differences exist within the general body of material and in the pottery that is associated with it. It seems probable that the Nok artwork represents a style that was adopted by a range of iron-using farming societies of varying cultures, rather than being the diagnostic feature of a particular human group as has often been claimed.

Just as the Nok terracottas had a problem with archaeological context that made their interpretation difficult, so also did the sculptures of Ife, in south-western Nigeria, although for a different reason. This body of art, as famous as that of Nok, also resulted mainly from accidental discoveries but from generally shallow sites that were covered by a thriving modern city. Building and other activities have repeatedly uncovered lost-wax castings (Chapter 19) of brass or copper and numerous terracottas but the condition of many of the items and the character of the deposits in which they have been found suggests that, like the Nok terracottas, they were not in their original positions. It seems that many of them had been accidentally discovered previously and placed in shrines, which had subsequently collapsed and become buried, while some had been repeatedly dug up for use in religious ceremonies and then reburied. Nevertheless, there was no denying the major importance of the Ife artwork. Many people were impressed by its apparent naturalism, here were the metal and terracotta heads of real people and animals. However, the Ife heads may appear naturalistic but they are actually idealized representations rather than portraits. Furthermore, although the style and technique of the art could be examined, the major questions concerning its context remained problematic for some time: who made it, for whom did they make it, what was its purpose, and when was it made?

Gradually, answers to these questions have been found. First of all, the artwork was clearly produced by highly skilled specialists, some working in

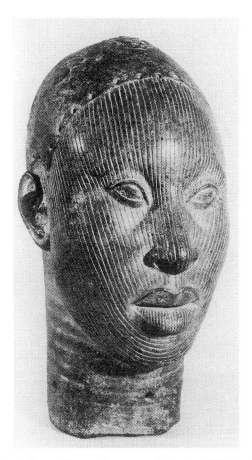

Figure 47 Brass head from Ife, south-western Nigeria. Height 30.5 centimetres. Reproduced by permission of Frank Willett from Willett, F. 1967. *Ife in the history of West African sculpture.* Thames and Hudson, London, Plate 3.

clay to produce the often delicately finished terracottas that must have been so difficult to fire successfully, others modelling in wax and then casting in brass or copper. So distinctive is the style of the Ife sculptures and, with some exceptions, so confined to the Ife area, that the specialists must have been ancestors of the Yoruba people who still live in that area. Specialists need time to learn their skills, however, and need economic support while they practise them. In short, they need patrons, which will inevitably mean that they produce what the patrons want. Many of the Ife sculptures are of human heads, often life-sized or a little less, heads wearing crowns or, in the case of some of the metal ones, shaped so that separate crowns could be fitted onto them. Some of the metal heads also have rows of holes most likely for the attachment of beards and moustaches and some have facial scarifications. Furthermore, most of the metal heads have holes in their necks, where they have been attached to something. From all this it seems most probable that the heads were fitted onto life-sized wooden bodies, that were dressed to resemble the deceased and carried at 'second burial' ceremonies, which occur because of the necessity to bury the real body soon after death. Yet these must have been no ordinary second burials but those of the elite, the ancient rulers of Ife and members of their family, both men and women. Additional evidence that the artists were mainly working for the elite is provided by smaller-scale metal castings depicting whole figures, that are represented wearing crowns and dressed in fine clothes and beads.

However, terracotta artwork is more common than that of metal and has a greater subject range. There are, indeed, terracotta human heads of great sensitivity, some of which appear to have formed parts of near life-sized bodies but other heads were clearly meant to stand on shrines. Moreover, the terracottas also include representations of domesticated and wild animals and include some items apparently made by less skilled artists. Indeed, a close examination of the art of Ife shows how varied it really is. Not only were there metal and terracotta sculptures but there were also some of stone, usually in quite hard material. Several of these were ceremonial stools, carved out of quartz or granite, others represented human figures and fish, or were slender standing stones of which the best preserved is the approximately 5-metre-high Opa Oronmiyon near the centre of Ife. Some of these stone carvings are decorated in a most unusual way, with spiral-headed iron nails that have been driven into drillings in the stone, so that only the head shows. Clearly blacksmithing skills were also well developed in ancient Ife, as is clearly demonstrated by a pear-shaped lump of wrought iron weighing over 50 kilograms preserved in one of the shrines. This remarkable object must have been painstakingly built up by forging together many separate pieces of iron. In addition, the repeated discovery of crucible fragments coated in variously coloured glass suggests that glass-working was practised, probably for bead-making, even if the glass was not actually made in Ife. The character of many of the terracottas also hints at the former existence of a woodcarving tradition, for which the direct evidence has not survived, although the spirited Yoruba woodcarvings of recent times probably derive from it.

As for the date of the Ife sculptures and their social and economic context, archaeological excavations have been particularly helpful. According to radiocarbon dates, Ife was already occupied over 1000 years ago and the sculptures date variously to between about 1000 and 500 years ago. During this period Ife grew into a city surrounded by defensive earthworks, and with its occupants living in mud houses of a distinctive plan, many of which had floors of broken pieces of pottery set on edge. Within the houses were shrines, on which some of the sculptures must have stood, representing deities and ancestors. The city had a ruler with both sacred and secular power, in recent times called the Oni. Although basically supported by an agricultural economy, the location of Ife near the northern edge of the rainforest suggests that much of its apparent wealth must have come from controlling trade with adjacent savanna peoples. With the subsequent development of the Yoruba city of Old Oyo further north, Ife lost that control and declined in importance. Nevertheless, it remained of great religious significance to the Yoruba people, whose traditions claim it as the place where the world was created.

Finally, an extreme example further demonstrates the importance of the archaeological context of ancient sculpture. In the Cross River area in the far

Figure 48 Carved stone in the Cross River area, eastern Nigeria. Height 84 centimetres. Reproduced by permission of the National Commission for Museums and Monuments, Nigeria, from Allison, P. 1968. *Cross River monoliths.* Department of Antiquities, Federal Republic of Nigeria, Plate 42.

east of Nigeria are some 295 carved stones. Varying in size from less than 0.5 to almost 2 metres high, with some weighing nearly 400 kilograms, these are natural boulders which have been carved with human features and other details. They are striking and sometimes fearsome images that presumably represent deities or ancestors. Yet almost nothing is known about their context, except that they are assumed to have been carved by the predecessors of the Ekoi people of the area. It is thought that they probably date to various times during the last 500 years, although the excavation of a pit near one of them produced a radiocarbon date of nearly 2000 years ago, the relevance of which is unclear. Thus they remain, ancestral faces from the past, glowering at us as they keep their secrets.

21

BENIN CITY

From forest power to world fame

Benin City, in southern Nigeria, is famous throughout the world. This is because of the existence of many items of Benin art, which over the last hundred years have become scattered through museums and art galleries in numerous countries. The art is of a distinctive style and consists of large numbers of brass castings showing extraordinary technical skill, ivory objects which have been carved with great delicacy, and objects of carved wood, wrought iron, and various other materials. Amongst the world's art collectors, Benin art is extremely valuable and there is probably more of it in countries outside of Africa than there is even in Nigeria, where it actually came from. More important than the art itself, however, are the developments that it represents. If we ask who made it, and why and how and when they made it, then we uncover a remarkable story of how a group of people became one of Africa's most powerful forest states.

Benin City is situated in the Nigerian rainforest, some way to the west of the delta of the Niger River and inland from the coast. It should not be confused with the Republic of Bénin, which lies to the west of Nigeria and used to be called Dahomey. At first sight the location of Benin City is difficult to understand. It is not situated on the coast nor on a major river, and to people not used to a rainforest environment it seems an unlikely place for a city to grow up. Yet grow up it did, starting probably about 1000 years ago and, because it could only be approached along easily defended narrow paths through the dense vegetation, its forest location probably helped to protect it from attacks by neighbouring peoples who envied its success.

That success was based on the skill with which the numerous resources of the rainforest were exploited. This environment was more varied than would appear to outsiders and farming was highly productive. Well-drained areas of better soil and less dense vegetation were cleared and planted, although after use for a few years they had then to be abandoned for a long time to recover their fertility. Yams and oil palms were particularly important sources of food but a variety of other crops were also grown, to which more were gradually added after their introduction from the Americas over the last 500 years. Domesticated animals were less important because they quickly died of a disease spread by the tsetse flies that were common in the area. However, many centuries of exposure to this disease resulted in some cattle and goats developing a resistance to it. Also meat could be obtained from hunting in the forest, and the rivers and creeks of the area contained plentiful fish. In addition, the forest provided other useful resources: wood for building, canoe-making, carving, and so on; leaves for roofing; creepers for making rope; plants for medicines; clay for pot-making; ivory for carving or trading; and many other things.

People had been living in or near the Nigerian rainforest for thousands of years before the growth of Benin City. Stone tools and pottery excavated from the rock-shelter site of Iwo Eleru, some distance to its north-west, demonstrate this, as do stone axes that have been found in Benin City's more immediate neighbourhood. However, the development of iron-smelting in this part of Africa from about 2000 years ago, and the production of iron tools, must have made the exploitation of the forest much easier and led to the expansion of many farming communities. It seems that by about 1000 years ago these were increasingly competing with one another, especially in the area north of where Benin City later grew up. Land was plentiful but, because each part that was farmed needed so long to recover its fertility, every settlement had to control a much larger area than was needed for food production at any one time. As a result, the occupants of each settlement dug a ditch and constructed an earthen bank around the territory that was thought essential for their support. After a few hundred years there was a very large number of these enclosed areas, of different sizes and shapes and adjacent to one another. The network of enclosures covered an area of about 6500 square kilometres of forest and forest margins in southern Nigeria, a part that was occupied by people who spoke a language called Edo. The earthworks of which the enclosures consisted have been estimated to have a total length in excess of 16,000 kilometres and to have required at least 150 million person-hours to construct. Only powerful motivation could have caused such an enormous effort and it seems likely that there was increasing conflict between individual communities, each within their laboriously con-structed boundary. Groups of settlements probably formed alliances for mutual benefit, and strong leaders of these alliances emerged from amongst the most successful warriors.

Much of the above is a reconstruction of what may have happened, because we do not know the actual events that took place. Nevertheless, it was in some such fashion that one particular community or group of communities came together to form the beginnings of Benin City. By 700 or 800 years ago people were already living there, and had probably been there for some time. A little over 500 years ago the inhabitants constructed an exceptionally massive earthen bank and ditch around the city for defen-sive purposes. Measuring at least 17 metres from the bottom of its ditch to the top of its bank and with a circumference of more than 11 kilometres, it would have taken five dry seasons for 1000 labourers, working for ten hours a day, to construct it. The successful completion of such a project suggests direction by a powerful centralized authority and by this time Benin City was indeed ruled by a king known as the Oba of Benin. He provided leadership in military, religious and civil matters.

A whole series of chiefs was responsible to the Oba for running the city and the increasingly numerous communities outside the city which were subject to it. Within the city were numerous craftsmen, many of them working for the Oba, who cast brass, carved ivory, worked iron, and manufactured objects of wood and other materials. There was also a flourishing pottery industry, probably in the hands of women. In addition, the inhabitants were expert in the construction of mud buildings, many of which were finely finished with polished red walls decorated with horizontal grooves. The Oba's palace and the houses of the more important chiefs had high-pitched shingled roofs and a plan in which rooms were arranged around a series of rectangular courtyards left open to the sky. Before about 500 years ago some of these buildings also had floors of broken pieces of pottery set on edge in mud, a type of paving that suggests cultural links with the Yoruba city of Ife, where it was in use at a similar or earlier date.

This description of Benin City about five centuries ago has been put together from several sources that cross-check one another. First, there are the remains of its earthen defences, and beneath the ground have been found traces of its buildings and examples of its handicrafts. Next, there are the traditions of its past that have been handed down over many generations, recording the names and exploits of its Obas, of their chiefs, their allies and enemies, their wars, and so on. It is claimed that these traditions reach back about 1000 years but because of the passage of time they are probably less reliable for the earlier periods. Nevertheless, they were carefully remembered by chiefs who were given that particular responsibility and one of whom (Jacob Egharevba) wrote them down in recent times. Finally, there are the numerous accounts of European visitors, who first came to Benin City over 500 years ago. Portuguese, Dutch, French, British and others, they were traders, missionaries, explorers, sailors, soldiers, government officials, and so on, who left records of what they saw. They were impressed by the size and organization and power of Benin City. Some of the earliest European visitors used guns to assist the Benin army in its conflicts with neighbouring peoples, and others tried, unsuccessfully, to convert the Benin citizens to Christianity.

Most of the European visitors to Benin City were interested in trading, however. From Benin City they could get peppers, ivory and slaves, and as time went on they became particularly interested in palm oil from the numerous oil palms that grew in the area. In exchange they brought a great variety of manufactured goods, especially textiles and metal items. They quickly found that amongst the things sought after by the inhabitants of

Figure 49 Excavation through some 700 years of occupation deposits at the old site of the Oba's palace, Benin City. In the left corner can be seen the top of a narrow shaft over 13 metres deep, near the bottom of which was a mass sacrifice of at least 41 young women.

Benin City were copper and its alloys brass and bronze. The local people were already familiar with these, having previously obtained them by trade with the interior. They were also familiar with the technique known as lost-wax casting, in which a wax model of the object to be cast is enclosed in clay which is then heated to expel the wax, after which molten metal is poured into the hollow mould. Using this technique and with greatly increased supplies of copper alloys from European traders, the metal craftsmen of Benin City very much expanded their production between about 500 and 100 years ago, continuing at a reduced level down to recent times.

Most of the examples of Benin art preserved in collections around the world were probably made during the last few hundred years before the Colonial period but the origins of the art go back much further in time. Many of the finest pieces were expressly for the use of the Obas or their most senior chiefs and seem to have been intended for both religious and other purposes. Life-sized brass castings of human heads represented the fathers, grandfathers, and so on, of the Obas and other important people, and were placed on altars used in rituals that honoured such ancestors and at times included human sacrifices. Large elephant tusks, elaborately carved, in some cases were stood upright in holes in the top of these brass heads, and also featured in religious ceremonies. Many other castings also had a religious

Figure 50 Brass head from Benin City, about 300 years old. Height 23 centimetres. Reproduced by permission of Cambridge University Museum of Archaeology and Anthropology, accession number: CUMAA 1902.95.

function but some may have been intended to provide a record of Benin history. Writing was not introduced in Benin City until the Colonial period, beginning about 100 years ago. Until that time it is likely that some of the works of art served as memory aids in the task of remembering the traditions of the city and its growing state. This was particularly the case with a large series of cast brass plaques: flat, rectangular pieces of metal about the size of a large open book. At one time these were fixed to some of the walls in the Oba's palace, and on them are detailed representations of Obas, chiefs, soldiers, servants, musicians, buildings, animal sacrifices, even Europeans with their muskets and other weapons.

Warfare seems to have been a dominant theme in the history of Benin City. At the height of its power, around 400 years ago, it appears to have controlled a large part of what is now central southern Nigeria. Thereafter its importance declined, as the effectiveness of the Oba's rule was increasingly impeded by

129

complex ritual and by the ambitions of his chiefs. The problems that resulted were partly responsible for bringing Benin City into violent conflict with the expanding colonial power of Britain about 100 years ago. Benin's defeat and subsequent looting led to the dispersal of thousands of items of art across the world but in the end defeat became a triumph. Benin City ceased to be a West African forest power but instead achieved world fame.

22

POTS AND PEOPLE

Early farmers south of the Equator

A university student commenting on a particular archaeological course once remarked that it was all about pots but one was never told about the people who made the pots. Such a criticism reveals one of the most difficult tasks faced by archaeologists: that of using physical evidence to tell a human story. A notable example of this problem is the investigation of the first farming societies in Africa south of the Equator, for which the bulk of the evidence consists of pottery, often in a fragmentary state. Partly because of poor conditions of preservation, partly because of inadequate research methods, the evidence for other aspects of life, such as subsistence economies, metallurgical knowledge, and social organization, is far more limited. As a result, the main focus of research has been on the similarities and differences amongst pottery from a large number of sites, spread over a huge area of central and southern Africa. This has been in spite of archaeologists being unable to agree about what variations in shapes and decorations of pots might tell us concerning the people who made and used them. It has been necessary to concentrate on the archaeological pottery evidence because the relevant period of roughly 2000 to 1000 years ago is too remote for oral tradition to be of help and there are no written records. However, important information has been obtained from the languages of the area, whose study does enable us to see something of the people behind the pots.

For over a century it has been realized that there are close similarities between the languages spoken by many millions of people south of the Equator. From this it has been argued that these languages have developed from a common ancestral language and that this development took place only during the last 2000 years or so. A common word in these languages is *bantu*, meaning 'the people', and the name 'Bantu' has therefore been adopted to describe this group of similar languages. It has been assumed that the area where Bantu languages show the greatest diversity must be where the common ancestral language originated. That area is thought to have been in the far north-west of the present distribution of these languages, most probably in what is now central Cameroon. From there, it is thought that Bantu languages spread to the south-east and south into

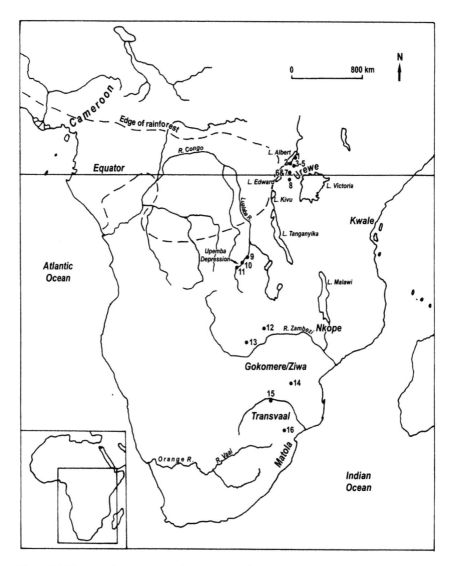

Figure 51 Farmers in central and southern Africa: important pottery groups, sites and areas. Refer to Chapters 22–24. Numbered sites are: 1. Kibiro. 2. Kibengo. 3–5. Munsa, Mubende Hill and Kasunga. 6 and 7. Ntusi and Bigo. 8. Bweyorere. 9. Kamilamba. 10. Sanga. 11. Katoto. 12. Kapwirimbwe. 13. Kalundu. 14. Great Zimbabwe. 15. Mapungubwe. 16. Lydenburg. Map by Sue Singleton.

central and southern Africa, a development that has been called 'the Bantu expansion'. They have been spoken in recent times by farming societies with a knowledge of metallurgy, and these languages have long contained words concerned with cultivation, herding, and the working of metal, some of which are thought to have been borrowed from speakers of the Central Sudanic languages to their north. In contrast, surviving hunter-gatherers in the southern half of Africa have been speakers of Khoisan languages. It has therefore been thought that the practice of farming and the production and use of metals were adopted throughout much of central and southern Africa following the arrival of people speaking Bantu languages. It has been assumed that actual migrations took place, although of a slow-moving form as slash-and-burn cultivation necessitated the exploitation of new land, but the process was probably complex, involving existing people as well as migrants.

Thus the linguistic evidence provides us with a glimpse of real people, the Bantu. The question is whether we can identify them in the archaeological evidence. The only such evidence plentiful enough for this to be attempted is pottery. By studying the geographical distribution of its various types, and using the radiocarbon method to date the sites where they have been found, an attempt can be made to identify the groups of people who introduced farming and metallurgy to Africa south of the Equator. With the addition of the more limited evidence for other aspects of their material culture, it is then possible to gain some idea of what their life was like. The oldest of these groups is that called by archaeologists the Urewe, which was situated to the north and west of Lake Victoria between about 2500 and 2000 years ago. Characterized by pots with a depression in their round base and distinctive incised and grooved decoration on their shoulder and rim, this group smelted iron and, although the evidence is very limited, they seem to have kept cattle and to have cultivated finger millet and sorghum. It is thought that they originated from people who had gradually moved through the savanna north of the equatorial rainforest, from the Bantu homeland in West Africa, in the process adopting farming and metallurgy from speakers of Central Sudanic languages with whom they came into contact.

By a little under 2000 years ago pottery comparable with that of the Urewe group was being made in what is now south-eastern Kenya and north-eastern Tanzania. It has been used by archaeologists to identify another group of people that they have named Kwale. It is apparent that farming societies, or at least their practices, were spreading and this process continued in a southerly direction for several centuries, resulting for instance in the Nkope group south-west of Lake Malawi, the Gokomere/Ziwa group of the Zimbabwe Plateau, and the Matola group of southern Mozambique and Natal. Similarities of pottery over a distance of more than 3000 kilometres and a period of only about two centuries suggest a rapid expansion of

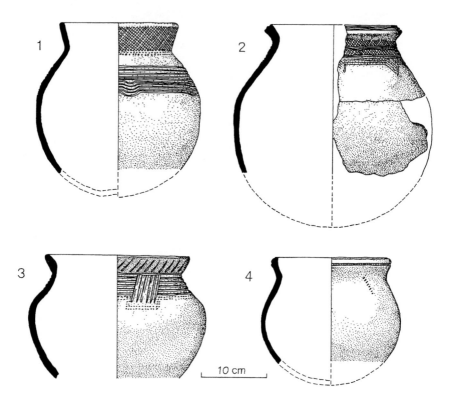

Figure 52 Pots made by early farmers in central and southern Africa. 1. South-western Kenya. 2. Northern Zambia. 3. Southern Malawi. 4. North-eastern Transvaal. After Phillipson, D.W. 1977. The spread of the Bantu language. *Scientific American* 236(4), Page 112.

farming and metallurgy, although the movement of individual groups must have been slow and intermittent. Thus the archaeological evidence provides some confirmation of the linguistic evidence, suggesting that major economic and technological change was brought about by the spread of people with similar material cultures, who spoke closely related languages. This overall movement, which affected eastern and central Africa from Lake Victoria to the Transvaal, has been called the 'eastern stream' of the Bantu expansion.

This term distinguishes the Urewe and related groups from others to their west, who had different pottery and have become known as the 'western stream'. Less is known about these groups but it has been suggested that they comprised Bantu-speaking peoples who moved south from their Cameroon homeland, along the Atlantic coast as far as northern Angola. They might also have migrated along savanna corridors opened up through the equatorial rainforest during a dry phase, or along its many rivers, and some possibly resulted from subsequent interaction with Urewe people moving to the west around the southern margins of the rainforest. It is thought that the earliest of these western groups were still using stone artefacts and it is uncertain when they adopted farming. Nevertheless, about 1500 years ago it was groups of the western stream that brought both farming and metallurgy to what is now south-eastern Democratic Congo and western Zambia. In the former place they were to give rise to the remarkable developments in the Upemba Depression that are the subject of Chapter 23; in Zambia they included the Kapwirimbwe and Kalundu groups. By this time the groups of the two streams were coming into contact in central Zambia and northern Zimbabwe.

Distinguishing human groups on the basis of the characteristics of their pottery is only a beginning. We also need to know what their subsistence economy and technology other than pottery was like, and what their social organization was. However, in these matters it has to be admitted that our knowledge of early Bantu people is limited. For instance, considering that these were the first farmers in a huge part of the African continent, we know little about their cultivation and herding practices. From such evidence that has been found, it seems that pearl millet, finger millet and sorghum were the principal crops, and that Bambara groundnuts, cowpeas and gourds were also grown. The conditions required for these plants restricted the settlement of early cultivators, in particular excluding drier areas to the west and south. However, the herding of livestock made it possible to exploit a greater range of environments, in which sheep, goats and cattle could be grazed. Amongst groups of the eastern stream, sheep and goats, particularly sheep, seem to have been more numerous than cattle, although the latter (probably both humpless and humped) became the most common by about 1000 years ago. In contrast, some groups of the western stream appear to have concentrated on cattle from an earlier date, although those in equatorial rainforest environments must have had a rather different economy: depending mainly on yams, oil palms and other useful trees, and keeping dwarf goats. In addition, it is likely that many early farming groups benefited from the introduction of South-East Asian plantains, bananas, yams, rice, sugarcane, coconut and citrus fruits, at least 1500 to 2000 years ago. Somewhat later and with a similar origin were chickens, although they were already in Egypt over 2000 years ago.

Important in the technology of early farming groups in central and southern Africa was their knowledge of metallurgy. The smelting and forging of iron provided tools that must have contributed significantly to the spread of cultivation. Nevertheless, destructive tropical soils and the probably high value of the metal have resulted in few of them being found. Most common are small items such as jewellery and arrowheads but furnace remains and other evidence of smelting suggests that iron production was extensive.

Jewellery was also made from copper and in Zimbabwe gold was being mined more than 1000 years ago. Other aspects of technology for which there is some evidence include salt production and house construction, the latter using frameworks of sticks plastered with mud and roofs of thatch.

Social organization seems to have been based on relatively small villages, often located in areas with soils suitable for cultivation. The increasing importance of cattle as time went on probably influenced the layout of these settlements, so that houses were arranged in a circle around a central cattle enclosure, as was common in later times, but the antiquity of this practice is uncertain. However, it is apparent that cattle came to play an increasingly important part in people's lives. They almost certainly figured, for instance, in the rituals and spiritual beliefs of early farmers. Some indication of these is provided by the unique series of life-sized terracotta human heads found at Lydenburg, in the eastern Transvaal. Significantly, one of these heads is surmounted by a representation of a domestic cow.

From about 1000 years ago the material culture of Africa south of the Equator became increasingly diverse. This was reflected in the form and decoration of the pottery which became more varied and more regionally distinctive. In many areas cattle gradually became the basis of wealth and power, underpinning social and political developments such as those at Mapungubwe, in the extreme north of South Africa, and at Great Zimbabwe, sites that are discussed in Chapter 26. There was also a substantial growth in trading connections, particularly with the East African coast. Nevertheless, there was an essential continuity from the previous early farming period. There was also a continuing interaction with the hunter-gatherer groups who still occupied extensive areas, particularly in southern Africa. Far to the south, in the Cape Province of South Africa, for instance, almost 2000 years ago hunter-gatherers began to herd sheep and to make their own quite distinctive pottery, and cattle-herding was also eventually adopted. Many farming communities, for their part, supplemented their diet by hunting and in some cases continue to do so till the present day.

The spread of farming into Africa south of the Equator is one of the world's major human achievements and yet it is one that was unknown less than a century ago. Even now many of the details are uncertain but we have at least the outline of a story about real people who spoke a group of related languages and whose endeavours brought about major economic and technological change. It is a story about the people who made the pots that archaeologists have studied but without the pots we would have known much less about the story.

23

THE TESTIMONY OF THE DEAD

Life in the Upemba Depression

Archaeologists have sometimes been criticized for excavating the graves of the dead, an aspect of their research in which the views of the living have to be given sympathetic consideration. Such investigations are necessary because of the important information about past periods that can be obtained from the study of human remains and of the objects often buried with them. This is particularly the case in areas where settlement or other activity sites yield only limited information. Such an area is the Upemba Depression, in south-east Democratic Congo, where most sites of the last 1500 years have only shallow deposits that have been heavily disturbed by subsequent human activity but where there are large numbers of burials of the same period clustered in cemeteries. Over 300 graves have been excavated in six different sites. They have provided most of the evidence for this period of human occupation in the area. It is apparent that during this time considerable economic, technological, social and political developments took place in this part of central Africa, relatively remote from influences from outside the continent. These developments culminated in the emergence of the Luba state, on whose origins before recent centuries both written sources and oral traditions are silent. Thus the investigation of the dead has provided important information about life in the Upemba Depression during a crucial period of its human history.

Although over 500 metres above sea level, the Upemba Depression is a relatively low-lying area with mountains to its north-west and south-east. It is occupied by a series of lakes and by the Lualaba River, a major tributary of the River Congo. Much of the area is subject to seasonal flooding, making cultivation more productive than in the surrounding savanna, which provides grazing for domestic livestock. In addition, the lakes, the Lualaba, and other rivers provide a major source of fish and in the past there was an abundance of both land and aquatic animals for hunting. To these advantages were added the availability of important raw materials in or near the area. Both iron ore and salt could be obtained and, to the south-east, was one of the richest and largest copper deposits in the world, extending from the extreme south-east of present-day Democratic Congo into what is now northern Zambia. Following the arrival of iron-using farming people in the Upemba Depression, it is hardly surprising that the area became densely populated and was the location of major cultural developments in the past.

The earliest farmers in the Upemba Depression seem to have been part of the so-called 'western stream' discussed in Chapter 22. Excavations at Kamilamba, at the northern end of the valley, yielded an occupation level with pottery, iron artefacts, grinding stones and palm nuts but no copper. Pieces of hardened mud with reed impressions were also found, suggesting the sort of houses that were constructed. Radiocarbon dating indicated that this evidence belonged to a period commencing about 1500 years ago. The site at Kamilamba has been used by archaeologists to name the earliest period of farming settlement in the Upemba Depression, that has been called the Kamilambian. Its people seem to have had cultural affinities with others both to the west in Democratic Congo and Angola and to the east in northern Zambia. In the latter area copper was already being mined and smelted on a small scale but its use was confined almost entirely to the region of production.

The next period, called the Early Kisalian after Lake Kisale in the northern part of the valley, seems to have developed from the Kamilambian. It has been dated to a little over 1000 years ago and is known from a relatively few graves. These contained iron hoes, knives and spearheads, as well as pottery and rare copper objects, mainly bracelets and anklets. Ceremonial iron axes, with engraved and perforated blades and nail-studded wooden handles, were found in two of the wealthiest graves, suggesting the emergence of local leaders. In one of these graves, as well as a number of pots, there was also a cylindrical iron anvil which, like the axes, was a traditional symbol of authority amongst Bantu peoples. The excavated evidence suggests that the population of the area was still fairly small and scattered but the presence of copper items indicates that the Upemba Depression was becoming part of a trade network, to which fish was probably its main contribution. Because of its colour and the ease with which it could be worked, copper became highly valued in much of Africa over the centuries.

From the Early Kisalian there developed the period known to archaeologists as the Classic Kisalian, commencing about 1000 years ago and lasting for several centuries. Evidence for this period consists of numerous graves in sites spread across the northern half of the Upemba Depression. The size and number of the sites suggests that there was a significant growth in population at this time. Excavations have been conducted on five sites belonging to this and the other related periods, of which Sanga is the most important. Collectively, Classic Kisalian burials have yielded an impressive range of grave-goods as well as informative skeletal remains. There were numerous iron objects, including hoes, knives, axes, arrowheads, spearheads, harpoons, fish hooks, necklaces, pendants and chain. There was an abundance of copper items, both ornaments such as belts, necklaces and bracelets, and utilitarian

Figure 53 Classic Kisalian burial at Sanga, south-eastern Democratic Congo. Note the many pots and the iron, copper, snail-shell, animal bone and ivory items indicated by the numbers. Reproduced by permission of Pierre de Maret from de Maret, P. 1977. Sanga: new excavations, more data, and some related problems. *Journal of African History* 18(3), Plate I.

things such as small knives, spearheads and fish hooks. There were also bracelets and necklaces of finely carved ivory. In addition, there were many pots of a high quality and a distinctive style. The grave-goods differed depending on the sex of the deceased, and their quantity and character apparently varied with the wealth or status of the individual, of which even some children's graves showed evidence. Burial practices appear to have been complex, the depth of burial depending on the age of the individual, adults being buried deeper than children and children deeper than infants. Burial was usually in an extended or slightly flexed position, on the back or on the side, with the feet downstream to the Lualaba River. Some of the superb pottery was evidently made specially for funerary use, being too small for practical purposes and in children's graves of a size proportional to the age of the deceased. Apparently contemporary with Classic Kisalian society were other people who were in the southern half of the Upemba Depression and had a different but related material culture. Only one of their sites has been excavated, at Katoto, where burials revealed that in many cases a man was buried with women and children, a practice rare amongst Kisalian people. However, in both Katotian and Classic Kisalian burials there were some-times status symbols such as iron ceremonial axes, anvils, bells, and cowries from the East African coast. Indeed, in some graves at Katoto there were also other marine shells and glass beads.

Clearly, the societies identified by archaeologists as the Classic Kisalian and the Katotian represent a peak of cultural development in this part of central Africa. That the underpinning economy was basically agricultural is indicated by the iron hoes and grinding stones found with some burials and by the bones of goats and chickens. The evidence also shows that antelopes, elephants, hippopotami and crocodiles were hunted but the major element of subsistence was undoubtedly fishing. This is apparent from the presence of harpoons and fish hooks amongst the grave-goods and also from the fish bones found within some of the pots with the burials. Amongst those pots there were also some whose rims had vertical extensions to support another pot, apparently braziers for cooking fish in canoes, as is still the practice. Indeed, the major activity in the Upemba Depression remains fishing, which also provides its principal export. It seems likely that it was the high intake of protein from fish, and the variety of food from other sources, that led to an increased density of population in this region and was a major factor in its remarkable cultural development.

Without doubt, the most impressive aspect of that development, as wit-nessed by the excavated grave-goods, was technology. Metal-working, of both iron and copper, was clearly sophisticated, producing weapons, tools and items of personal adornment, by hammering and wire-drawing tech-niques. The carving of ivory also indicated a high level of technical ability, as did the quality of the pottery. In addition, it is likely that there existed a range of skills using organic materials which have not survived. Impressions

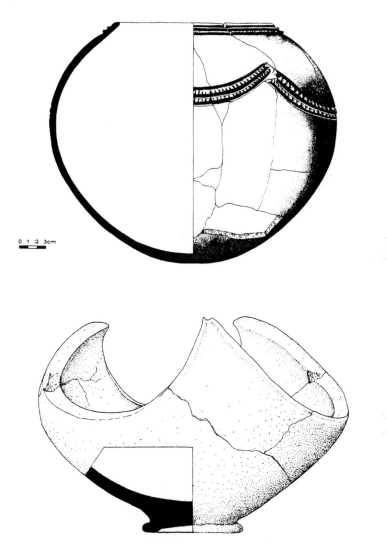

Figure 54 Kisalian pot (above) and pottery brazier (below). Reproduced by permission of the Royal Museum for Central Africa, Tervuren, Belgium from de Maret, P. 1992. *Fouilles archeologiques dans la vallée du Haut-Lualaba, Zaire, III: Kamilamba, Kikulu et Malemba-Nkulu, 1975. II: Planches.* Musée Royal de l'Afrique Centrale, Tervuren, Belgique, Planche 7. Nenquin, J. 1963. *Excavations at Sanga, 1957.* Musée Royal de l'Afrique Centrale, Tervuren, Belgique, Figure 20.

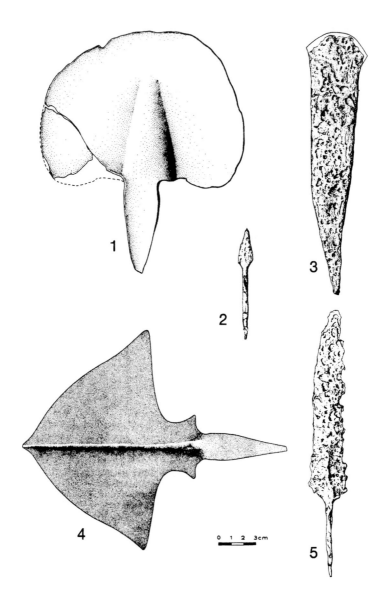

Figure 55 Iron tools and weapons from the Upemba Depression. 1. Hoe. 2. Arrowhead.
3. Axe. 4. Ceremonial axe. 5. Spearhead. Reproduced by permission of the
Royal Museum for Central Africa, Tervuren, Belgium from (1 and 4) de
Maret, P. 1992. *Fouilles archeologiques dans la vallée du Haut-Lualaba, Zaire,
III: Kamilamba, Kikulu et Malemba-Nkulu, 1975.* II: Planches. Musée Royal
de l'Afrique Centrale, Tervuren, Belgique, Planche 37/1 and Planche 23/1.
(2, 3 and 5) Nenquin, J. 1963. *Excavations at Sanga, 1957.* Musée Royal de
l'Afrique Centrale, Tervuren, Belgique, Figures 21/6, Figure 30/2 and 30/3.

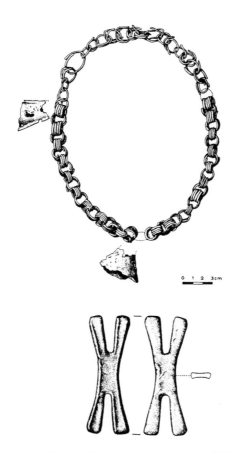

Figure 56 Kisalian copper chain and iron bells (above) and Kabambian copper cur-
rency cross (below). Reproduced by permission of the Royal Museum for
Central Africa, Tervuren, Belgium from Nenquin, J. 1963. *Excavations at
Sanga, 1957.* Musée Royal de l'Afrique Centrale, Tervuren, Belgique,
Figure 61 and Figure 21/1.

in corrosion on some of the metal items amongst the grave-goods, together
with some pots imitating baskets, suggest that basketry was amongst those
skills. Overall, the technology of the Classic Kisalian was one of the most
remarkable in tropical Africa during the period in question. It has been
claimed that it indicates the presence of professional craft-workers.

However, it is the social and political implications of the excavated evidence that are the most important and the most interesting. It is apparent
that the people of the Classic Kisalian period belonged to an hierarchical
society, with chiefs probably wielding both political and ritual power,
beneath whom others were ranged according to wealth and status. Judging
from the sophistication of the material culture and the strength and

continuity of its burial traditions, the period seems to have been one of political stability and good order. As such, it can be regarded as an early stage in state development, although probably one in which boundaries were social and ritual rather than geographical and in which power was fragmented rather than centralized. The crucial point is that this development seems to have occurred in virtual isolation from the outside influences that have so often been claimed to explain such developments in other parts of Africa. The extensive use of copper in the Classic Kisalian indicates that by then a substantial trade had grown up with people mining it to the southeast but the few trade goods that reached the Upemba Depression from the East African coast, some 1500 kilometres away, suggest only indirect and minor contacts.

Some 700 years ago the Kisalian burial ritual changed: the grave-goods becoming less numerous and the pottery less elaborate. At the same time there appeared distinctive copper crosses, probably originally as ingots that changed hands as a trading commodity but later becoming a form of currency. This period has been called the Kabambian, after Lake Kabamba at the northern end of the Upemba Depression. It has been divided by archaeologists into Kabambian A and Kabambian B, on the basis of further changes about 500 years ago in burial practices and pottery, and a tendency for the copper crosses to become much smaller and their size more uniform. This probably marks a change from their use as a special-purpose currency (for instance, to buy wives) to a general-purpose one, that would have needed smaller units of more uniform size. The use of such a currency would imply the development of an increasingly centralized political authority and, indeed, the apparent end of the Kabambian B period about 200 years ago is at the very time that the Luba state emerged according to oral traditions. It came to exercise control over a large area of savanna south-east of the central African forest. By that time the Upemba Depression had developed wide inter-regional trading connections, and the presence of cowries and glass beads in Kabambian B graves indicates increasing contact with the Indian Ocean coast.

The capitals of the Luba state were located outside of the Upemba Depression, to its north-west, but it appears that the state originated in the Depression itself. Its archaeology has provided a record of human endeavour extending over 1500 years, which presents a remarkable story of continuity and change in which the origins of the state can be seen. Furthermore, the excavated skeletal material compares closely to that of later Luba people. Thus the burials of the Upemba Depression have provided a rare insight into social and political development in central Africa. Without the testimony of the dead we would know almost nothing about a vibrant period of Africa's past.

24

'ONE BEAUTIFUL GARDEN'

Production and power amongst the Great Lakes

Travelling in Uganda a century ago, the young Winston Churchill called it 'from end to end one beautiful garden'. A few decades before, it was the political development of the area that had most impressed its earliest European visitors. They had previously known nothing about Bunyoro and Buganda and the other states that they found in this part of central Africa. Since that time the question of how such developments had taken place has been a major focus of research into the past of the Great Lakes region. Part of the explanation probably lies in the very thing that made such an impression on Churchill. The region is rich in natural resources and potentially highly productive. Although its settlement by early farmers over 2000 years ago (Chapter 22) seems to have been patchy, the population appears to have grown in size and density after about 1000 years ago. A resulting competition for resources probably led to an unequal distribution of wealth, so that a few individuals were able to gain power over many others. This would have involved complex adjustments within the societies concerned but fundamentally it was probably the control of production from an abundant environment that provided the power base of the emerging states.

The Great Lakes region consists of the large area between Lake Victoria, on the east, and Lakes Albert, Edward and Kivu, on the west, nowadays comprising most of western Uganda, part of north-western Tanzania, and the countries of Rwanda and Burundi. Straddling the Equator but with a climate moderated in many areas by an altitude of more than 1000 metres, its temperatures and rainfall are generally high without being excessive. Together with relatively fertile soils in many areas, this has enabled the cultivation of a range of crops of which finger millet and bananas were the most important, each providing the staple food of specific parts of the region. In its cooked form, the vegetable banana known locally as *matooke* has been a basic part of the diet in areas of greater rainfall. In addition, in the drier parts of the Great Lakes region are some of Africa's best grasslands, often free of tsetse flies and the disease they carry, and able to support large numbers of cattle. Furthermore, the lakes and rivers have important supplies of fish, and both land and aquatic animals were formerly numerous enough to contribute significantly to human subsistence. The region also possessed raw materials of importance, iron ore, salt and ivory, whose exploitation provided valuable commodities for an extensive trading network, aided by transport on the lakes and rivers.

The developments that culminated in the states recorded by the first European visitors probably commenced some 1000 years ago. This is too long in the past for oral traditions to be helpful, and so it is to archaeological evidence that we must principally turn. Unlike the Upemba Depression (Chapter 23), this comes mainly from settlement sites rather than from burials but it is nevertheless often difficult to interpret. Linguistic research suggests that by about 1000 years ago the early farming societies of the region were already changing as cattle and bananas increased in importance. The most valuable archaeological evidence for the period that followed comes from Ntusi, on the grasslands of southern Uganda. Occupied from about 1000 to 500 years ago, this was an extensive settlement that grew to a size of around 100 hectares. Most of its occupation deposits are shallow but excavation has produced large quantities of broken pottery, animal bones of which most are young cattle, numerous grindstones, curved iron knives thought to have been for harvesting cereals, burnt grain identified as sorghum, and storage pits probably for grain. There was also evidence for iron-working, fragments of ivory of which some were worked, beads made of ostrich eggshell, traces of circular houses, and glass and cowrie-shell beads indicating contact with the Indian Ocean coast during a late period. Thus the occupants of Ntusi seem to have been both herding cattle and cultivating sorghum and probably finger millet, a later division of these activities between a cattle-keeping elite and commoners who cultivated having not yet occurred. Archaeological survey in the Ntusi area located over 50 much smaller sites of a similar date, of which three were excavated, revealing both the remains of cattle and occasional evidence of cultivation. There was a lack of sites of intermediate size and it has been suggested that this settlement pattern indicates that Ntusi was a chiefdom but had not yet developed into a centralized state.

Indications that things were changing have come from the huge site of Bigo, only a few kilometres north of Ntusi. It consists of some 10 kilometres of ditches and banks, enclosing an area of about 5 square kilometres. The earthworks form two main enclosures, within the larger of which is a central group of smaller enclosures with three large mounds. Excavation has revealed that this central area was occupied by people with an economy based on cattle. The larger enclosures were unoccupied but look as if they were for penning cattle and perhaps for enclosing cultivation, rather than for defence. The height and width of the banks and ditches vary greatly but the greatest height from the bottom of the ditch to the top of the bank is over 7 metres and it has been estimated that more than 200,000 cubic metres of earth and rock would have been dug out in making the ditches as a whole.

Figure 57 Part of the inner ditch system, Bigo, Uganda, cleared in preparation for excavation. Reproduced by permission of Merrick Posnansky.

Collectively the evidence suggests the existence of a centralized society with an economy largely based on cattle and it is possibly significant that nearby Ntusi seems to have been abandoned after the development of Bigo some 500 years ago. Bordered on one side by the Katonga River, the latter site would have been a better location for cattle-keepers than the dry grassland area of Ntusi. A huge artificial depression near Ntusi, from which it has been estimated that almost 30,000 cubic metres of material have been removed and piled up, has been interpreted as a means of reaching the water-table in order to provide water for cattle. Although undated, its scale would suggest that it was created over a long period of time and that the need for water was extreme. In such circumstances, the abandonment of Ntusi in favour of Bigo might indicate that cattle, rather than a balance of cattle and cultivation, were becoming economically dominant and, indeed,

147

were bringing about changes in social and political organization. Bigo could have been the centre of an early state that lasted for several centuries, a predecessor of the states observed by the earliest European visitors nearly 150 years ago.

If this was the case, then it might have been one of a number of such early states because there are other earthworks in north-west Uganda. Best known are those at Munsa, north of Bigo, and Kibengo, near the southern end of Lake Albert, at both of which there has been some archaeological excavation. The earthworks at these sites were probably constructed at about the same time as those at Bigo, although like Bigo there is also evidence of occupation at an earlier date. The animal bones at Munsa were mostly those of cattle but at Kibengo there was a greater variety of animals represented. At Munsa there was also abundant evidence of iron-smelting, in the form of slag and other waste as well as the remains of a furnace. A rocky hill at the centre of the earthworks seemed to have been occupied before they were dug and several burials were found there as well as settlement and smelting debris. In spite of the overall similarity of the sites, differences between the evidence excavated from Bigo, Munsa and Kibengo are thought to indicate that they represent the centres of different competing states, rather than one single state with its capital at Bigo.

In an attempt to set such developments into their context, an archaeological survey was conducted in the Munsa area, revealing some 130 sites all belonging to the last 1000 years. Study of their pottery showed how early small sites had given way to sites that ranged in size, some of which were protected by earthworks. These developments were all prior to the emergence of the state of Bunyoro, perhaps only 300 years ago. This was one of the states observed by the first European visitors and there exist oral traditions that attribute its origins to a mysterious series of rulers called the *Cwezi*. Claims have been made of their association with a number of archaeological sites, some of which have shrines dedicated to these semi-mythical figures. Two of these sites have been partly excavated, Mubende Hill and Kasunga. The former produced evidence of two settlements, one about 700 years old and the other belonging to the last two centuries. The earlier was at most 5 hectares in area, had large amounts of animal bone dominated by cattle, and a number of possible grain-storage pits in which grinding stones were found. Kasunga yielded substantial occupation evidence, including possible grain-storage pits, numerous grindstones, and animal bones dominated by cattle but also from other species. In addition, there were several burials and the site was thought to date to no more than 400 years ago. Both Mubende Hill and Kasunga could indeed have played a part in the process of state emergence but both their role and that of the supposedly associated *Cwezi* remain uncertain.

Nevertheless, some places relevant to the later stages of state emergence can be identified. In Buganda and Bunyoro a number of royal tombs belonging to recent centuries have been preserved and in Ankole, in south-western Uganda, the sites of some of the former royal capitals are known from oral tradition. Excavations at one of these, at Bweyorere, revealed a large settlement for whose inhabitants cattle-keeping had been important and hunting rather less so. Although its houses had left no traces, there were remains of a large circular building, presumably of wood, mud and thatch, which was over 15 metres in diameter, and was interpreted by the excavator as a palace. Oral traditions indicated occupation of the site at three different periods during the last 400 years and radiocarbon dating was in general agreement with this overall time-span. Both glass beads and fragments of pottery smoking-pipes were found at the site.

Archaeological research has also shed some light on the antiquity of iron and salt production in the Great Lakes region. Along with ivory, these commodities must have played an important part in the development of regional trading networks, in a growth of contact with the Indian Ocean coast, and in the emergence of states. There is evidence that iron was being smelted in north-west Tanzania over 2000 years ago and in Rwanda and Burundi perhaps as much as 3000 years ago (Chapter 9). It is also apparent that salt

Figure 58 Salt production at Kibiro, Uganda. Earth, previously scattered on the ground to absorb salt, is scraped up prior to leaching and boiling the resulting brine.

was being made at Kibiro on the shores of Lake Albert by about 800 years ago and the later presence at this site of beads of glass and then of ivory, as well as cowrie shells, suggests developing contact with the distant East African coast.

The origin of states in the Great Lakes region remains inadequately understood. They appear to have emerged by about 300 years ago as the culmination of a sequence of social transformations that commenced some centuries earlier. Fundamental to these changes was a highly productive subsistence economy based on grain and banana cultivation and cattle-raising. As time went on there seems to have been more and more emphasis on cattle, that came to represent not only wealth but also ritual and political power for those increasingly elite members of society who owned large numbers of them. Political power enabled control to be extended over more negotiable commodities such as iron and salt, to which ivory and slaves were later added to meet the demands of the Indian Ocean trade, a trade that eventually brought the Great Lakes and its states to the notice of the outside world. Thus it appears to have been the phenomenal productivity of the region that provided the fundamental basis of power.

25

FACING TWO WORLDS

The trading settlements of the East African coast

The people of much of the East African coast are different from their inland neighbours and have long been so. Five centuries ago, when Portuguese seafarers first rounded the southern tip of Africa and entered the Indian Ocean, they found a coastal society that was largely urban, mercantile, Islamic, and partly literate, with extensive maritime contacts. In contrast, most of the peoples of the adjacent interior remained farmers, pastoralists and hunter-gatherers, with their own African forms of religion. The inhabitants of the coast occupied a narrow strip fronting the ocean, stretching from southern Somalia to southern Mozambique, some 3500 kilometres. They also occupied a number of offshore islands, as well as the Comoro Islands and parts of Madagascar. In time, they became known as the 'Swahili', because most of them were and are speakers of ki-Swahili, a north-eastern Bantu language rich in loan-words from Arabic and other languages, but it is uncertain how long this name has been in use. Nevertheless, it is clear that many of the settlements of the coast and islands existed for a very long time, although often eventually abandoned. Collectively, various Arabic and even Chinese writers indicate their presence back to about 1000 years ago, and Greek sources suggest an origin almost 2000 years ago. The major problems have been to explain how such a development took place and to identify the people who contributed to its unique character.

Because the East African coast formed a contact zone between the Indian Ocean and the African interior, its inhabitants were facing two very different worlds. It was their adjustment to this situation that allowed them to become intermediaries, who could profit from participation in some of the most important international trade before modern times. The advantageous situation in which they found themselves basically resulted from environmental factors. Unlike the west coast of Africa, the east coast benefited from the monsoon winds, which for half the year blew from the north-east and for the other half blew from the south-west. This enabled sailing vessels to reach East Africa from southern Arabia, the Persian Gulf and the west coast of the Indian subcontinent, and to return to their ports of origin within a year. Furthermore, seasonal reversal in the direction of the main currents in the Indian Ocean made voyages possible from even further away, as is demonstrated by the apparent arrival of Indonesian immigrants in Madagascar over 1000 years ago. In addition, the East African coastal environment also contributed to the cultural developments that took place. With fringing coastal islands and an offshore coral reef, much of the coast offered sheltered anchorages or sandy beaches where the lightly built sewn boats that were used could be run ashore on the high tide and unloaded or loaded at low tide. In short, this was a coast whose characteristics encouraged the use of seaborne transport, both along the coast itself and to overseas destinations.

It was also a coast that was relatively rich in natural resources and therefore able to support a substantial population. A maritime tropical climate with adequate rainfall, together with some areas of fertile soils, particularly in the lower valleys of the mainland rivers, enabled much of the coast to be agriculturally highly productive, although its drier northern part was less fortunate. Sorghum and millet were probably the most important crops that were grown and cattle, sheep, goats and other domestic animals seem to have been raised. The introduction of a number of South-East Asian plants, such as bananas, sugar cane, Asian rice and coconuts, a consequence of the coast's overseas contacts, must have further strengthened the local economy, although it is uncertain when they arrived. Also this was a coast rich in fish and other marine foods and wild game was plentiful in the African hinterland. As well as food, there were other important resources, such as timber from the coastal forests for general construction and shipbuilding, and mangrove poles, much used in building, from the coastal swamps. Sources of iron ore made it possible to smelt and forge iron on a substantial scale. The coral reefs and outcrops of coral on dry land provided both building stone and lime for mortar and plaster. In addition to coconuts, the various species of coastal palms supplied wine, rope, matting and caulking for ships. Locally grown cotton was used in textile manufacture and even silk was produced. Salt could be evaporated from sea water and some marine shells were used for bead manufacture and other decorative purposes. Finally, fresh water could be obtained from wells even in settlements close to the sea.

However, it was not coastal resources but those of the African interior that were the main reason for the phenomenal mercantile success of the coastal settlements. Quite simply, the coastal traders could obtain substantial quantities of several commodities that were keenly sought by the Indian Ocean trade. These were ivory, gold and slaves, and not only did the coastal traders obtain these but they controlled the supply. To these commodities, they could also add other African exotica that were highly marketable in either Asia or Europe, such things as rhinoceros horn and tortoiseshell, frankincense and myrrh, ambergris and sandalwood, rock crystal and ebony. Furthermore, the coast was able to supply commonplace materials that were much needed in the desert lands of Arabia and the Persian Gulf, such as mangrove poles and grains. In exchange, the coastal traders received fine ceramics from the Arab world and even from as far away as China, as well as glassware, beads of glass and semi-precious stones, and other luxuries, but the biggest import was probably cloth, particularly high-quality materials. This was because the trading cycle that developed was not just a straight-forward exchange of African goods for imported manufactures. There were actually four categories of goods: those from the African interior for export, those imported from overseas for trade with the interior, those (particularly luxuries) imported for use in the coastal settlements, and commodities pro-duced in those settlements for trade with the interior. Thus, the larger of the East African coastal settlements became places where goods were collected, bulked and distributed, as well as exported and imported. In the process, the settlements prospered and their merchants became wealthy.

The oldest archaeological evidence for international trade was found at Ras Hafun, in northern Somalia, where ceramics were excavated that had come from the Red Sea, the Persian Gulf and perhaps South Asia, a little over 2000 years ago. Somewhat later in date are four Roman glass beads from Mkukutu in the Rufiji delta of Tanzania and two fragments of Roman pottery from Unguja Ukuu on the island of Zanzibar; these and other sites indicating that small coastal settlements were already participating in over-seas trade. Indeed, by 1100 to 1400 years ago such trade had reached the site of Chibuene in the far south of Mozambique and of Dembeni in the Comoro Islands, both of which contain imported ceramics. However, such evidence must be seen in context. There are no reliable discoveries of Roman coins from the East African coast, although at a later date Islamic, Indian, Sri Lankan and Chinese coinage reached it. Furthermore, as continued to be the case in later periods, the imported ceramics formed only a small part of the pottery excavated from the coastal sites, the bulk of it being locally made African wares. The earliest of the latter is of similar appearance on many widely distributed sites and seems to have evolved from pottery made by some of the region's first iron-working farming communities. Thus it seems that the origins of the coastal trading communities were African but other elements in those communities were introduced from outside Africa and the difficulty is to determine when and how this occurred and from where those external inputs came.

The introductions included at least some settlers from the Persian Gulf and the Arabian coast but most importantly they included the religion and cultural practices of Islam. Neville Chittick, who excavated the urban sites of Kilwa, in Tanzania, and of Manda, in Kenya, argued that a substantial immigration had taken place, as some of the oral traditions of the coast claim. However, excavations by Mark Horton at Shanga, also in Kenya, sug-gested a more gradual process of change in which the African coastal people played a major role. For instance, the earliest settlement at Shanga appears to have been pre-Islamic and both the central mosque and the later stone

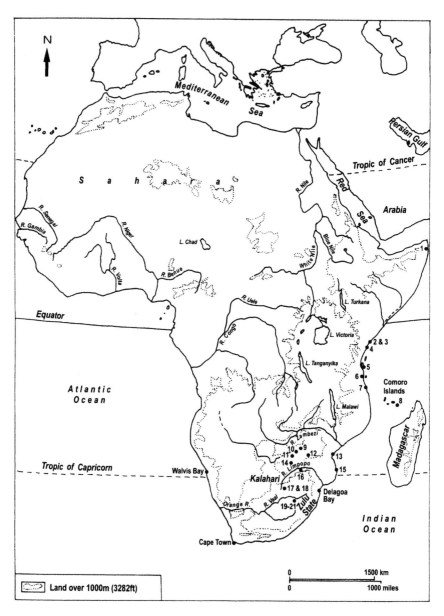

Figure 59 Important later sites and places in east and southern Africa. Refer to Chapters 25–27. Numbered sites are: 1. Ras Hafun. 2 and 3. Shanga and Manda. 4. Gedi. 5. Unguja Ukuu. 6. Mkukutu. 7. Kilwa. 8. Dembeni. 9. Naletale. 10. Danangombe. 11. Khami. 12. Great Zimbabwe. 13. Sofala. 14. Toutswe sites. 15. Chibuene. 16. Mapungubwe. 17 and 18. Kaditshwene and Molokwane. 19–21. Ntsuanatsatsi, Makgwareng and Matloang. Map by Sue Singleton.

houses seem to have developed from humble timber, mud and thatch predecessors. These and some other coastal settlements grew from modest African
origins, a little over 1000 years ago, into the cosmopolitan towns and cities
that the Portuguese encountered about 500 years later. Certainly these
places experienced numerous alien influences from the Indian Ocean trading
world but to varying extents they appear to have been absorbed by the predominantly African population, which itself was subtly changed in the
process.

The East African coastal communities were at their most successful
between about 800 and 500 years ago. One of the more important was the
city of Gedi, in Kenya, where substantial stone ruins remain and where excavations have been particularly informative. There were fine stone houses for
the elite, with latrines, washplaces and drains. There were wells, stone-built
mosques and tombs, a large building complex that was interpreted as a
palace, and a city wall within which there must also have been many poorer
dwellings of timber, mud and thatch. The stone houses are similar to those
in many other coastal settlements, of which some built in the last few centuries are known to have housed leading merchants, whose privilege and
power they displayed.

Gedi, like Kilwa, Manda and Shanga, was one of the larger and more
important of the coastal settlements. There were many others, many also
with stone ruins, but they varied greatly in size from cities of more than 15
hectares to hamlets of only 1 hectare. The question is, how did they relate to
one another? Is it possible to talk about a state made up of these various
communities? Certainly there were individual rulers of some of the larger
cities, some of them even minting their own coins and one of them building
the fine palace of Husuni Kubwa, near Kilwa, with its bathing pool, domed
and vaulted roofs and Arabic inscriptions. However, documentary records
and coastal traditions from the last few centuries indicate that in later times
the governance of coastal communities varied greatly, often including coun-
cils of prominent people and sometimes having no individual ruler at all.
The situation prior to Portuguese contact is difficult to assess but it seems
unlikely that any single kingdom or other form of state developed. Rather
there seems to have been what might be expected of essentially mercantile
communities, intense competition between individual cities or towns, who
controlled lesser settlements in their vicinity. At best the coast consisted of a
complex pattern of city states, which not surprisingly fell an easy prey to
Portuguese ambitions and still later to the Omani Sultanate of Zanzibar.

On several occasions almost 600 years ago giraffes were presented to the
Emperor of China. They had come from the east coast of Africa and represent perhaps the clearest demonstration of the extent and capacity of the
Indian Ocean trade, in which the East African settlements were able to
participate. By means of that trade, those settlements made important contributions to world markets and, as we shall see in Chapter 26, their trading

Figure 60 A giraffe from East Africa at the court of the Emperor of China almost 600 years ago. Reproduced by permission of the British Institute in Eastern Africa from Sutton, J.E.G. 1990. *A thousand years of East Africa*. British Institute in Eastern Africa, Nairobi, Page 69.

activities also had repercussions deep in the African interior. The communities that lived along the coast consisted basically of African people but their trading activities brought visiting merchants and even some settlers from the northern coasts of the Indian Ocean and brought new ideas about religion and behaviour, ideas usually expressed in the Arabic language. The result, over many centuries, was that there emerged a distinctive coastal people, now known as the Swahili, with their own unique culture and a language that provides mutual understanding through much of East Africa. This was the consequence of standing between Africa and the outside world, influenced by both and benefiting from both.

26

PROJECTING POWER

Great Zimbabwe and related sites

One of the most remarkable and certainly one of the best known archaeological sites in Africa is Great Zimbabwe, a site which has even given its name to the country in which it is situated. It lies near the south-eastern edge of the Zimbabwe Plateau, an area of high land much of which is over 1000 metres above sea level. To the north and south of this plateau are two of the continent's major rivers, the Zambezi and the Limpopo, to the east is the wide coastal plain of the Indian Ocean and to the west the Kalahari Desert. The elevation of the plateau makes it a relatively attractive place for human settlement and between about 1000 and 500 years ago it was the location of important developments, of which Great Zimbabwe was the most outstanding consequence. As the first large city of the southern African interior and controlling much of its surrounding area, it also participated in the Indian Ocean trade handled by the mercantile settlements of the East African coast (Chapter 25). For perhaps two centuries it was the most powerful centre in its region, a power that was physically expressed in the monumental stone structures which have made it famous. To understand how this came about, it is essential to examine the rise and fall of Great Zimbabwe in its full context: geographical, chronological, social, economic and political. In the past, Great Zimbabwe was sometimes presented as a great mystery but the only mystery is why it should ever have been thought to be one.

The environment of the Zimbabwe Plateau and its surroundings presented both opportunities and constraints for human settlement. For much of the plateau the climate was relatively temperate, with a moderate seasonal rainfall. The altitude ensured freedom from tsetse flies, that rendered much of the coastal plain and adjacent river valleys unhealthy for both domestic animals and people. A vegetation cover varying from wooded savanna to grassland provided abundant grazing, particularly for cattle. Easily cultivated soils, of which some were quite fertile, could produce a variety of crops, sorghum and millets being the most important in the past. The plateau also possessed, or had access to, a number of other resources, including iron, copper, gold, tin, salt and soapstone, as well as clays suitable for building and others suitable for potting. In addition, the granite that outcropped in many places provided an easily exploited source of building stone. Furthermore, wild game was plentiful and could supply supplementary food or, in the case of elephants, a valuable raw material in the form of ivory.

Such advantages inevitably encouraged population increase amongst early farming communities but they also had to face a number of constraints. The rainfall of the plateau was notoriously unpredictable: it could arrive too late, be too heavy, or most seriously fail completely. On average, one in every five years faced such difficulties, drought being a particularly severe problem, with locusts and other pests further complicating the situation. Thus famine and its associated diseases were a constant threat. In addition, many of the plateau soils were of short-term fertility, necessitating the continual abandonment of cultivated areas after several years so that they could revegetate and recover. Therefore, successful cultivation and adequate harvests required frequent labour-intensive clearing of new land or of land that had lain unused for some years. Drought and varying soil fertility affected livestock as well, limiting water sources and grazing and making seasonal and other movements necessary.

Ethnographic and documentary sources from recent centuries suggest how the farming peoples of the Zimbabwe Plateau were able to adapt to this interplay of opportunity and constraint. When famine threatened, their livestock, particularly their cattle, could either be eaten or traded with other more fortunate communities that still had a supply of grain. For these and other reasons, cattle became of major importance, representing wealth as well as an insurance against bad years. Also communal action, regarding which land to plant, when to plant, where to graze livestock and so on, had to be coordinated; a task that ultimately fell to the head of each descent group, a man who was regarded as the controller of the relevant land on behalf of the ancestors. As such he had important ritual knowledge and power, and was expected, when necessary, to be able to make the rain fall. It was probably such social and ritual developments that eventually led to the social complexity represented by urban growth and state formation, of which Great Zimbabwe was the principal example. As the heads of their descent groups, these men could not only amass wealth in the form of cattle and grain but also control any materials which could be traded either locally or to more distant markets. In return, they could obtain other commodities whose redistribution amongst their groups could further strengthen their position.

The earliest archaeological evidence of developments of this sort is provided by the Toutswe sites of eastern Botswana, that date from about 1400 to 700 years ago. Situated in prime cattle country, large herds were built up by the occupants of settlements that ranged in size from 1000 to 100,000 square metres. These settlements seem to have had little trading contact with the outside world but by about 1000 years ago similar developments in the Limpopo Valley show that trade was already established with the Indian

Ocean coast. This was a trade in which ivory and gold were exchanged for glass beads and probably for other goods which have not survived archaeologically, such as cloth. Most remarkable of the Limpopo sites is Mapungubwe, situated in the extreme north of South Africa. At its greatest development, almost 800 years ago, this was a settlement probably exceeding 240 hectares in size, with a population of 3000–5000. Located on a flat-topped hill surrounded by steep cliffs, Mapungubwe had elite housing and high-status burials containing items of gold. Many of the ordinary people seem to have lived at the base of the hill and collectively the site clearly represents an urban development. Indeed, considered in the context of comparable but smaller sites in the same area, it seems likely that Mapungubwe was the centre of a state that predated that of Great Zimbabwe. About 700 years ago it was abandoned, perhaps due to a deterioration of its already dry climate. Significantly, this was also at a time when Great Zimbabwe, situated in a more favourable agricultural area and closer to the sources of gold, was rising to prominence.

Great Zimbabwe appears to have originated as a small farming settlement, perhaps as early as 1700 years ago, and the earliest stone walls were not built until about 1000 years ago. Between then and about 500 years ago it grew into a city which at its peak had a population of about 18,000. The impressive drystone walls, which have attracted so much attention, were actually enclosures for the houses of the elite, buildings that although of mud and thatch were of the highest quality. The stone structures, whose plans are characterized by random curved forms, are in three main groups: a series of interconnected enclosures on top of a steep-sided hill, a large enclosure in the adjacent valley, and various smaller enclosures also in the valley. Most remarkable is the large enclosure in the valley, the outer wall of which is 244 metres long, up to 5 metres thick, 10 metres high, and has an estimated 5151 cubic metres of stonework made up of over a million carefully trimmed blocks. The top of this wall has a band of distinctive chevron decoration, consisting of stones set at an angle to each other. Within the enclosure is a conical tower, about 5.5 metres in diameter and over 9 metres high, built of solid drystone masonry. These and other features of the remarkable stone structures at Great Zimbabwe were clearly meant to impress the beholder with the power and wealth of a ruler and his supporters who could produce such monumental work. As for the rest of Great Zimbabwe's inhabitants, they lived in areas of densely packed small mud and thatch huts, whose total extent dwarfed that of the elite stone structures.

A major problem is to determine the basis of the power and wealth displayed by Great Zimbabwe. Its agriculture seems to have been strong, with cultivable soils in the vicinity and with large numbers of cattle and other livestock, for which lowland grazing was accessible during the dry season if plateau resources failed. Great Zimbabwe appears also to have had considerable ritual significance for the Shona (Karanga) people who built it. The

Figure 61 The conical tower in the large valley enclosure at Great Zimbabwe. Over 9 metres high, it shows a remarkable mastery of drystone masonry technique.

Figure 62 A stepped doorway in the hill-ruin at Great Zimbabwe. The curved stonework is characteristic.

main reason for its success, however, seems to have been its participation in long-distance trade, both within the African interior and with the trading settlements of the Indian Ocean coast. Commodities that were traded internally probably included iron tools and weapons, copper, salt, gold and some of the numerous glass beads obtained from the coast. Other goods from the coast included Persian and Chinese ceramics, fine glassware and metalwork, and almost certainly large quantities of cloth. In exchange, the coastal traders received gold, ivory, copper, slaves and various African exotica, that were probably taken down the Save valley to the Sofala area, about 400 kilometres east of Great Zimbabwe. Sofala trade appears to have been controlled for a time by Kilwa far to its north, and a coin from the east coast found at Great Zimbabwe was minted in Kilwa.

Although the biggest and most impressive, Great Zimbabwe was only one of a large number of similar settlements on the Zimbabwe Plateau and its fringes. At these places there were comparable, although smaller, stone enclosures, and the pottery and other aspects of material culture were the same. In addition, there were small settlements that lacked stone structures but seemed nevertheless to be related. From this evidence it has been concluded that Great Zimbabwe was the centre of a state, comparable perhaps to the kingdom of Monomatapa, that succeeded it to its north and which was recorded by the Portuguese on their arrival in the area about 500 years ago. By that time, Great Zimbabwe had already lost much of its power and the number of its inhabitants was very much less. The reasons for this decline are unknown but a downturn in the fortunes of the east coast trading settlements also occurred prior to the Portuguese arrival, probably as a result of changing market conditions overseas. Furthermore, by then the Zambezi valley was becoming the main route for trade goods from and to the coast, cutting Great Zimbabwe off from the major source of its wealth, perhaps because the gold sources that it controlled were becoming depleted. In addition, it is possible that the demands of its large population brought about an environmental collapse in the city's vicinity, as soil fertility declined, grazing deteriorated, and firewood and other resources became exhausted.

However, many elements of the culture of Great Zimbabwe lived on, particularly to its west in the Torwa state, where the major settlements of Khami and Naletale also had monumental stone structures, although these were in the form of highly decorated revetments rather than free-standing walls. Still later, in the same area, the Changamire (or Rozvi) state continued the stone-building tradition, for example at its capital Danangombe, until less than 200 years ago. Then the turmoil triggered by the rise of the Zulu state far to the south brought new people to the Zimbabwe Plateau, to be followed eventually by British colonization. By that time, a little over 100 years ago, the circumstances that had led to the rise of Great Zimbabwe were largely forgotten and have since had to be reconstructed by means of archaeological and historical research. Now the place is once again important, having become world famous. Its remarkable stonework still impresses visitors, as it was intended to do when built, still serving its purpose of projecting power.

27

DESERTED SETTLEMENTS WITH A STORY

Later farmers in southern Africa

The beginnings of farming in southern Africa over 1500 years ago have already been outlined (Chapter 22). Now it is worth examining it in a developed state as it existed for about the last 500 years, looking particularly at a region where mixed farming was most successful and gave rise to substantial social and political changes. Here 'southern Africa' is considered to be all of the continent south of a line drawn from the Limpopo River, in the east, to Walvis Bay, in the west. However, the western and south-western parts of this huge area were too dry to grow African cereal crops or had winter rainfall instead of the necessary summer rainfall. In those parts of southern Africa, livestock-herding or hunter-gathering or a combination of the two remained the subsistence strategies until European colonization over the last 300 or more years. In contrast, to the east and north-east both cultivation and livestock, particularly cattle, were important. This was especially the case on the highveld between the Vaal and Orange Rivers and some way north of the Vaal. In this area there are numerous deserted stone-built settlements belonging to the last few centuries. Their relatively recent date means that oral traditions, historical documentation and linguistic data can all help in the interpretation of their archaeological evidence, which consequently has quite a story to tell.

Geographers call this area temperate grassland, in South Africa it is referred to as the veld, a word meaning both grassland and open country. Indeed, the area is both of these things but it is also well over 1000 metres above sea level, so that it has a relatively cool and healthy climate. Certainly much of it is good grazing country for livestock. In addition, both rainfall and soil are generally suitable for cereal cultivation, sorghum and pearl millet formerly being grown but after about 300 years ago increasingly maize, which had been introduced from America. The latter can yield up to three times as much as the indigenous cereals and requires much less labour for its cultivation. However, it needs 25 per cent more rain and, in an environment prone to rainfall fluctuations and serious drought, this was to have disastrous consequences. The existence of such fluctuations is why livestock had become so important; cattle-keeping, in particular, helped to protect against food shortages, as well as providing a means of accumulating wealth and gathering supporters by loaning animals. In such circumstances, it is understandable that cattle became the centre around which life revolved, even dictating the layout of the settlements in which the farmers lived. Concerning this matter much more is known than usual, because most of the settlements were built largely in stone; specifically they included extensive drystone enclosure walls whose ruins are often still visible. This was another response to the grassland environment, for the general lack of trees meant that there was little wood available for building, it being reserved for the framework of otherwise mud-built houses and in some cases even these were built of stone. Such was the shortage of wood that dried dung had to be used for fuel in many places and iron tools and weapons had to be obtained by trade with other areas. Fortunately, in spite of the rounded character of much of the landscape, there were also convenient outcrops of rock that broke into pieces ideally suited for building. Settlements were often located on the ridges formed by such outcrops, giving ready access to building material as well as a commanding view of the surrounding plains.

Early farmers seem to have had little interest in the high grassland and it was probably only the increasing importance of cattle in their economy that led to substantial settlement in this area. However, a warmer, wetter period that provided more favourable conditions for cereal cultivation might also have encouraged increased settlement of this high country. Dating the earliest evidence for this is difficult but it was probably about 500 years ago. It was at this time that the earliest of the stone-walled settlements were built, each of them consisting of a cluster of settlement units with layouts known to archaeologists as Type N, after a site at Ntsuanatsatsi, in what is now the Orange Free State. These settlement units had a central ring of circular livestock enclosures which were connected by walling to form a large secondary enclosure, outside of which were houses of reeds and mud, the whole complex being surrounded by a low outer wall. Each settlement unit seems to have housed an extended family and its livestock; settlements being made up of as many as a hundred of such units, possibly containing up to 1500 people. However, these early settlements were widely spaced compared with later ones, suggesting that the overall population was still small. Excavation has produced broken pottery, clay figurines of cattle, iron and bone tools, bones of both domesticated and wild animals, stone platforms for grain bins, and indications that the houses were dome-like structures, sometimes with paved floors.

After some time, the layout of the individual settlement units changed to one that is referred to by archaeologists as Type V. Settlements consisting of units with this plan were much more common and more widespread than the earlier form and were located in areas with the best arable and grazing land. Each settlement unit was made up of circular enclosures of various sizes arranged in a rough circle and joined by connecting walls to form one

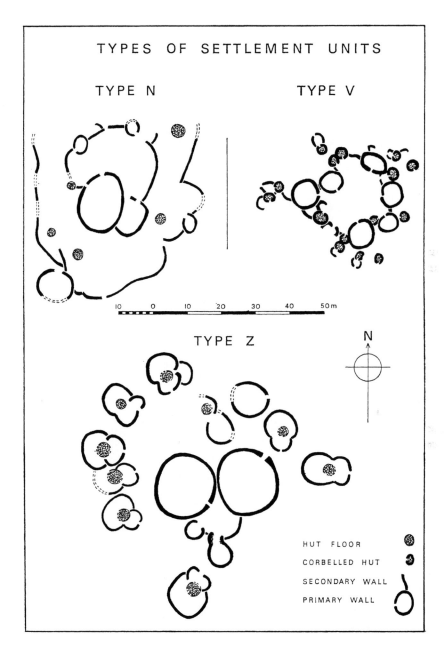

Figure 63 Settlement unit types on the South African highveld. Reproduced by permission of Taylor & Francis from Maggs, T. 1976. Iron Age patterns and Sotho history on the southern Highveld: South Africa. *World Archaeology* 7(3), Figure 16 (Journal web site http://www.tandf.co.uk/journals/routledge/00438243.html)

large enclosure. The outer wall of the Type N units was no longer present and the circular houses, which were sometimes of stone, were either in the open outside the large enclosure or formed part of the enclosure itself. Settlements comprising clusters of such units in some cases housed many hundreds of inhabitants. Occasional differences in the sizes of individual settlement units suggest that differences in wealth and power were developing within these communities. Furthermore, settlements were now closer together, indicating an increase in the overall population compared with the earlier period, and older settlements continued to be occupied or were reoccupied, stone from Type N settlement units often being robbed to build in the new style. Type V settlement units date from about 400 to less than 200 years ago and excavations at the settlement site of Makgwareng, in the present Orange Free State, have provided some information on the history of one of them. In this case the earliest occupants built enclosures of reeds, not stone, and constructed houses of mud-plastered reeds. Eventually these were replaced by five large stone enclosures that were linked to form a secondary enclosure, around which were six stone houses. In this form, the Makgwareng settlement unit was probably occupied by 18 to 45 people, comprising a family homestead, but subsequently additional houses were built suggesting that the number of occupants had increased. The end was apparently sudden and violent, with valuable iron tools and weapons abandoned at the site. Like many other settlements with Type V units, it seems to have been destroyed during the widespread warfare that engulfed this part of southern Africa almost 200 years ago.

In the north-west of what is today the Orange Free State was yet another design of settlement unit, that archaeologists have called Type Z. At the centre of each of these units was a compact group of circular enclosures for livestock and surrounding these were from 8 to 20 circular houses, often with front and back semi-circular courtyards. The houses were different from those of either the Type N or Type V settlement units. Apparently they had thatched conical roofs supported mainly by a ring of poles set outside of the mud wall of the building itself and thus providing it with a veranda. Again, these settlement units were grouped together into settlements, of which one particularly large example at Matloang has been surveyed and partly excavated. At that place, tightly packed houses and livestock enclosures extended for more than a kilometre along a ridge and might have had a population of over 1000 people. It has been estimated that such settlements were occupied a little over 200 years ago but the earliest of them might be 300–400 years old. When oral traditions, historical accounts and linguistic data are compared with the archaeological evidence, it appears that all three types of settlement unit were probably built by speakers of Sotho-Tswana languages but that whereas both Type N and Type V were the work of Sotho people, the first style developing into the second, Type Z settlement units were built by Tswana people. Thus it seems that the differences in layout amongst the stone ruins of the highveld actually reflect differences in its past populations.

A little after 300 years ago some Tswana settlements in the western Transvaal began to grow to a quite remarkable size, culminating in populations of 10,000 people or more. Kaditshwene appears to have been one of the largest, with a population almost 200 years ago of 20,000, making it the same size as contemporary Cape Town. Molokwane is thought to have been even bigger, a settlement 3 kilometres in length, averaging 1.5 kilometres in width and with an area of approximately 4–5 square kilometres.

Excavation of one of its smaller settlement units, covering an area of 1 hectare and loosely comparable in layout with the Type Z units, has provided a valuable picture of the life of its occupants. Over 79 per cent of the meat consumed came from domestic animals, cattle outnumbering sheep and goats, and there was evidence for the preparation of plant food including grain. In addition, the internal arrangements of the settlement unit shed light on the social structure of its inhabitants as well as on their daily activities. Considered as a whole, this huge settlement and others like it indicate an increasing centralization of economic and political power by local rulers, at least partly in response to growing instability. Population expansion,

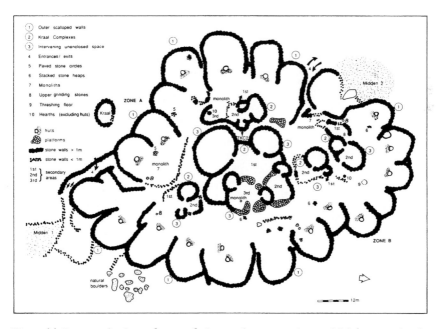

Figure 64 Excavated plan of one of the settlement units at Molokwane, in the western Transvaal. Reproduced by permission of Julius C.C. Pistorius from Pistorius, J.C.C. 1992. *Molokwane: an Iron Age Bakwena village*. Perskor Printers, Johannesburg, Figure 7.

partly fuelled by the introduction of maize, led to greater competition between chiefdoms for arable land and grazing and to more frequent cattle raiding as a means of augmenting wealth. In addition, the onset of drought made the situation even worse and the stage was now set for disaster.

Just under 200 years ago there erupted a series of wars and population movements that affected much of south-eastern Africa. Known as the *Mfecane*, meaning 'the crushing', this explosion of violence seems to have been principally sparked by intense competition for the control of resources, particularly those sought by European traders at Delagoa Bay, where the Mozambique port of Maputo now stands. Slaves appear to have been one of those resources but ivory was the principal one, as much as 50 tonnes (representing about 500 elephants) being exported each year, mainly in exchange for glass beads, cloth and brass. Such imports increased the wealth and power of those rulers who gained access to them and the competition for elephants grew ever more intense as they became more difficult to find. Add to this the effects of population growth and drought and the events that followed become more understandable. Out of the chaos emerged the Zulu state, centred in Natal, but for the settlements of the highveld the period has been remembered as the *Difaqane*, meaning 'the scattering', because the Sotho and Tswana people scattered and others scattered before them. As European settlers moved north in the years that followed, they found only deserted stone ruins, not the thriving communities of people and animals that had formerly existed.

These deserted settlements do indeed have a story to tell, a story that commences some 500 years ago although its early details are uncertain. However, for later times a clearer picture emerges, because archaeologists are able to use oral traditions, historical documents and language studies to assist in the interpretation of the physical evidence. It is only by putting together information from all these sources that we can begin to understand what the stone ruins have to say about the people who built them.

28

OUTSIDERS ON THE INSIDE
The impact of European expansion

Some parts of Africa have had contact with the outside world for a long time: in North Africa, in the north-east of the continent, and along much of the Indian Ocean coast. However, this was not the case for the western and southern coasts and most of the interior, where substantial external contacts only began to develop a little over 500 years ago, as Europeans ventured further and further from their own shores. In the centuries that followed, this European expansion was to have profound consequences for the lives of African peoples: fundamentally changing many aspects of their cultures. European commercial enterprise sought raw materials, cheap labour, new markets, and even land, culminating eventually in the colonial domination of almost the whole continent, a situation from which Africa has only emerged in relatively recent times. For this long series of developments there are copious documentary and oral records and a very large amount of historical writing based upon them. The material record has been given far less attention and the archaeology of recent times in Africa, historical archaeology as it is often called, is still a fairly new area of research. Nevertheless, its great potential is already apparent, providing not only an opportunity to improve our understanding of the European impact on Africa but also enabling us to see how Africans reacted to that impact.

At first, Europeans came to explore and to trade. In order to protect their commercial interests, they established trading posts that were often armed, partly as a defence against possible African attack but mainly against European competitors. The earliest of them was the 'castle' of Elmina, on the coast of what is now Ghana, built by the Portuguese over 500 years ago before the first voyage of Columbus to the Americas. Soon after its establishment, it was exporting an average of 20,000 ounces of gold a year, and as time went on first the Dutch and then the British gained control of it. In addition to gold, ivory and slaves were the main commodities sought by the earlier European traders on this coast, with the export of slaves to the Americas eventually growing to enormous proportions. Such was the competition that by about 300 years ago there were some 25 major trading posts and numerous smaller ones along about 400 kilometres of coast. They belonged

169

to Portuguese, Dutch, English, Danish, Swedish and German interests. Elmina Castle, modified over the centuries, survives as one of Africa's most impressive historic buildings but significant structures also exist at some other places. Excavations on the site of the town that grew up near Elmina Castle have shown how the local African population adapted to the presence of this alien establishment. The excavation of a dungeon at Cape Coast Castle has revealed the conditions in which African slaves were kept, prior to their shipment across the Atlantic. On the other side of the continent, Fort Jesus, at Mombasa, was also built by the Portuguese to protect their commercial activities but a century later than Elmina and it eventually fell into first Arab and then British hands. Excavations there and at the nearby underwater wreck site of a 300-year-old Portuguese frigate have provided valuable information about early European trade on this coast.

Trade inevitably led to settlement, often as a means of controlling commercial activities and sometimes involving people of mixed European and African descent. Such were the Portuguese *prazos* that were established along the Zambezi River, commencing almost 400 years ago and leaving distinctive archaeological traces. Intended as trading posts and agricultural estates, they gradually became more like African chiefdoms than Portuguese settlements, run by powerful families with their own private armies and a substantial share in the slave trade. A little over 100 years ago the most troublesome *prazo*, at Massangano in what is now Mozambique, had to be stormed by a Portuguese army. More successful in the long term was the Dutch settlement at the Cape of Good Hope, originally established 350 years ago to supply Dutch ships on their way to and from South-East Asia. Although not intended as an attempt at large-scale colonization, the settlement gradually grew into the city of Cape Town, where archaeological excavations have shed light on its development. European settlers also expanded into the adjacent parts of southern Africa, in the process dispossessing indigenous herdsmen and hunter-gatherers. Agricultural estates and farms were created, a notable example of the former about 300 years ago being at Vergelegen, east of Cape Town. Excavations have investigated a building that housed the slave workers at this estate, as well as a watermill/stable and a wine cellar. At the other end of the social scale, at about the same time, was the small military outpost of Oudepost 1, near Saldanha Bay, northwest of Cape Town. Life here must have been far from easy and the place was abandoned for a while following a partial massacre by the indigenous people of the area. Not surprisingly, excavations produced evidence of both a European and an African presence, indicating some of the interaction, peaceful or otherwise, that took place.

Inevitably, the growing European presence in Africa led to conflict, both between Europeans and Africans and between Europeans from different countries. As a result there is a considerable amount of archaeological evidence relating to military matters. For instance, over 120 years ago expanding

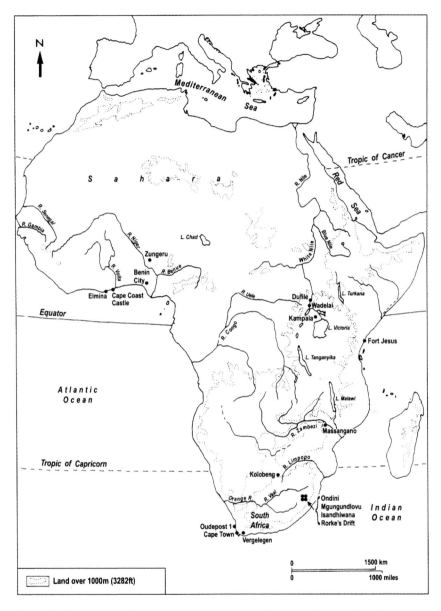

N

Mediterranean
Sea

Tropic of Cancer

S   a   h   a   r   a

R. Senegal
R. Gambia
R. Niger
L. Chad
R. Volta
Zungeru
Benin
City
R. Benue
Elmina Cape Coast
Castle

R. Nile
Red Sea

Blue Nile
White Nile

R. Uele
Dufile
Wadelai
Kampala
L. Turkana
L. Victoria

Equator

R. Congo
L. Tanganyika
Fort Jesus

Atlantic
Ocean

L. Malawi

R. Zambezi Massangano

Tropic of Capricorn
R. Limpopo
Kolobeng
Orange R.
R. Vaal
Ondini
Mgungundlovu
Isandhlwana
Rorke's Drift
Indian
Ocean
Oudepost 1
Cape Town
Vergelegen
South
Africa

0   1500 km
0   1000 miles

Land over 1000m (3282ft)

Figure 65 European and contact sites and places. Refer to Chapter 28. Map by Sue
       Singleton.

Figure 66 Part of Elmina 'castle', Ghana. Reproduced by permission of Christopher DeCorse.

European settlement in southern Africa collided with the expanding Zulu state. Belonging to this period are several sites of interest, such as the Zulu capitals and military headquarters of Mgungundlovu and Ondini, the first containing up to 7000 people and the second some 5000. Excavations have been conducted at both places. In addition, there are the battlefields of Isandhlwana, where the Zulu defeated a large British army, and of Rorke's Drift, where a small group of British troops repulsed a massive Zulu attack. Collectively, these sites provide a different perspective on a series of well-documented events. Less well known are the sites of forts built in northern Uganda over a century ago, such as Wadelai and Dufile on the upper Nile. Furthermore, individual relics of former conflict have sometimes survived, such as a 9-pounder Royal Naval gun, preserved in the Uganda Museum in

Kampala. Manufactured in London over 130 years ago, it was last in action against a German vessel on Lake Victoria during the First World War.

In contrast to their military involvements, Europeans also brought the Christian religion to large parts of Africa, although in several different forms. Missions, churches, cathedrals, hospitals and schools were built in many places and are material evidence of the endeavour of both Europeans and Africans. In some instances, the movement of settlements or the failure of enterprises means that earlier structures or their sites can be investigated. One example from 150 years ago is the site of the Kolobeng Mission, in Botswana, where the young David and Mary Livingstone struggled unsuccessfully for five years. Amongst the evidence identified at this place is the

Figure 67 Casualty of empire: a memorial at Namirembe Cathedral, Kampala, Uganda.

grave of their infant daughter Elizabeth, who died there. Such burials are, indeed, another aspect of the archaeological evidence for the European presence in Africa. Many earlier graves were not permanently marked and have been lost but in later times burial was usually in ground consecrated according to Christian rites and with an inscribed headstone. There are large numbers of such burials across the continent, from the neglected cemetery of the colonial headquarters at Zungeru, in northern Nigeria, to the carefully tended graves outside Namirembe Cathedral in Kampala, the capital of modern Uganda. Their inscriptions are an eloquent reminder of the European experience in Africa and of Africans' experience of Europeans. One of the Namirembe graves, for instance, is of a much-loved missionary whose headstone simply reads 'Mackay'. Apparently, nothing else was needed.

Some of the most important consequences of European activity in Africa were economic and technological. For instance, the subsistence economies of many African peoples were fundamentally changed following the introduction by Europeans of new crops from the Americas, of which maize and cassava were the most important but which also included tomatoes, tobacco and other things. On the technological side, the early introduction of firearms altered the character of war in the continent but during the colonial period, from about 100 to about 40 years ago, there were many other technological innovations of significance. These included the construction of railways and roads, the adoption of European building techniques, the development of mining methods, the use of the internal combustion engine, the generation of electricity, and a host of other introductions that originated from the industrialization of Europe itself. The archaeological study of such technological change has had little attention but some indication of its potential has been provided by the examination of the watermills, windmills and horse-mills of South Africa. They provide an intriguing example of technology transfer, commencing over 300 years ago. Mainly they were the consequence of the European settlers' preference for bread as their staple food, which made it necessary to grind grain into flour, a task for which power sources were limited. However, they were also used for sawing timber, grinding snuff, making sugar, raising water, and for driving mine-hoists. Watermills were particularly numerous and adhered closely to European designs, even including a number of the relatively uncommon type that has a horizontal waterwheel. As might be expected of settlers who in many cases had a Dutch background, windmills were also frequently constructed.

However, archaeological evidence of the European impact on Africa includes portable objects as well as structures and sites. Whether Europeans came to the continent for only short periods or came to settle, they brought much of their material culture with them or subsequently acquired it as imports. When such items are found in association with each other, they can be remarkably informative about past lives. Such a case was the Barrack

Street well in an old part of Cape Town, where a remarkable assemblage of things had fallen or been thrown into a well between about 200 and 100 years ago. Amongst the objects recovered were part of a leather belt, a wooden bucket, a doll's head, a door knob, hinges, thimbles, buttons, bottles, shoes, fragments of musical instruments, even two chamber pots and the skeletons of several domestic cats, as well as many other things. There were also cattle, sheep, pig and fish bones, and a large amount of broken crockery. Analysis revealed changes through time, showing for instance that at first Oriental ceramics had predominated, presumably because of the Dutch trading connections with South-East Asia, but that British material had subsequently become the most common, reflecting the British take-over of the Cape of Good Hope and the expanding production of British potteries.

Items of European origin have also been found in sites occupied by Africans, providing some idea of indigenous reactions to contact with Europeans. Fragments of alcohol bottles, clay tobacco pipes, glazed ceramic, glass beads, gun-flints and cowrie shells are amongst the more characteristic but a wide range of manufactured goods can also occur. Excavations in Benin City, in southern Nigeria, for instance, produced a selection of such material. However, the objects usually recovered give only part of the contact story. Amongst the most common trade commodities, for example, were textiles, which rarely survive in archaeological contexts. Nevertheless, the African response to Europeans and their goods is also apparent from other evidence. Thus, locally made clay smoking pipes are more common in West African sites than are the imported ones and amongst the famous brass castings from Benin are a number that depict European visitors but do so in an African way.

European expansion impacted on Africa as it did on so many parts of the world. In Africa, Europeans were outsiders but by trade, settlement and aggression they became to varying degrees part of the inside. More importantly, Africans adopted what suited them from what Europeans had to offer. The complex interaction that resulted and the outcomes of that interaction are just as susceptible to archaeological investigation as other aspects of human history. As yet such research is at an early stage but its potential is considerable. It provides an opportunity to study not just Europe's discovery of Africa but Africa's discovery of Europe and of things European.

29

REMEMBERING AFRICA'S PAST

During the last 100 years or so, much has been done by researchers to rediscover Africa's forgotten past. The previous chapters have merely sampled what is now known in order to give some idea of the progress that has been made. Any account of the human past must inevitably be selective and this is particularly the case when dealing with the whole of a large continent over a period in excess of 4 million years. The topics chosen here are those that stand out, like the areas lit by street-lights widely spaced along a darkened road. There are small highly illuminated patches which shade off into the shadows and there are stretches of intense darkness. This results from several factors, of which the most important is our sheer lack of knowledge of some areas and periods of time. It is hardly an exaggeration to say that what we do not know probably exceeds what we do know. For instance, the human story of the vast Congo River system is still very little understood compared with that of the narrow Nile Valley. Much more research by archaeologists, palaeontologists, historians and many others will be needed before such deficiencies can be remedied. In some cases this might take a long time, because particularly field research requires substantial funding and infrastructural support and can be difficult or impossible to conduct in areas that suffer from political instability or have serious health risks. Environmental conditions are also a problem, far less physical evidence surviving in the humid tropics than in the dry deserts, although this is a factor that has sometimes been exaggerated.

A further problem, that makes the telling of Africa's story so difficult, is the huge and diverse body of published literature to which the researcher and writer must give attention. Not only is it spread across a bewildering array of disciplines but it is so enormous that no single person can ever hope to read it all. In addition, there are very few libraries worldwide that can be said to hold a really comprehensive collection of it. As if all that was not enough, there is also the stranglehold of language to be considered. Relevant publications can be in a variety of languages, usually those of former colonial powers. Material in English or French is the most common but there is also Portuguese, Italian and German, not to mention other European languages from time to time. Add to these the sources that are in Arabic, Swahili or other African languages and it is apparent that any one person attempting to write about the whole of human history in the whole of Africa is either very courageous or very foolish. The usual solution has been to produce large books containing chapters by many different authors, each one of whom is a specialist in the field that she or he has written about. The result is often very impressive scholarship but difficult reading, a particular problem being the contrasting ideas and writing styles that such books often contain. Furthermore, books of that sort are usually very expensive and because of their specialist character attract only a limited readership. People should not need a university degree to be able to understand an account of their own heritage.

Indeed, the story of Africa's past is far too important for that and deserves to be known and appreciated not only in Africa itself but also in the rest of the world. Africa's role in world history has often been overlooked and yet, as the foregoing chapters have shown, we owe our very existence to the continent, which also made major contributions to the development of agriculture and to a variety of subsequent cultural transformations that have a relevance beyond its shores. An outstanding instance of this has been the impact of Ancient Egypt on Western society, both in the past and in recent times. Significantly, however, there has long been an implicit denial of the source of that impact, failing to accept Ancient Egypt for what it undoubtedly was, an African riverine civilization. Similarly, Africa north of the Sahara has repeatedly been treated as part of the Mediterranean world, rather than part of Africa as such. This tendency has been reinforced by those who have promoted the concept of what they have called Sub-Saharan Africa, by which means they have neatly beheaded the continent and concentrated on the parts that they happened to think of as being 'African'. Inevitably this raises questions about the concept of Africa as such, although there is surely as much justification for using it as there is for the widely accepted idea of Europe or Asia.

In spite of Africa's major contributions to the world, most people outside the continent continue to have little knowledge of them and, indeed, even within the continent there is only limited appreciation. As an archaeologist specializing in tropical Africa, the writer has spent many years trying to convince non-archaeologists that there really is something for archaeologists to 'find' in Africa. There remains a usually unspoken but deeply ingrained idea in Western society that nothing much happened in the African past and that therefore there is not really anything to look for. Fortunately, both Africans and non-Africans are increasingly writing about the continent's past and, together with film, television and the Internet, their publications are making relevant information more accessible to people in the so-called developed world. In Africa itself, however, such material seems to have had only limited impact, probably because economic conditions often prevent its reaching potential readers. Books are expensive and frequently universities, schools and private individuals cannot afford publications produced in Britain, America or elsewhere, or even if they can afford them are prevented from purchasing them by restrictive currency regulations. As a result, it can be difficult for the outcome of research to feed back to the very people whose societies it concerns. One consequence of this seems to have been a general lack of concern for cultural heritage, resulting in the looting of many archaeological sites in Africa and the theft of items from some of its museums. These activities are basically promoted by the insatiable materialism of Western society, which can turn even the past into a marketable commodity, but they are made possible because some Africans are prepared to sell their birthright. Cultural heritage is a vital part of a people's identity but this seems to have been forgotten.

This is surprising, particularly in view of the very substantial interest that now exists in the documentary and oral history of Africa, both within and outside of the continent. However, such history tends to be heavily loaded at the near end, that is to say that its emphasis is very much on the last few centuries. Given the socially and politically traumatic experience of colonization and decolonization, this is to be expected, just as it is understandable that the international slave trade should attract so much attention. Furthermore, the limited time-depth of most oral traditions inevitably tends to focus attention on more recent periods. Admittedly, the study and teaching of African history does give some attention to earlier periods in those areas that have a relevant documentary record, even if it is very sparse. However, Africanist historians have rarely made adequate use of the physical evidence that exists for those parts of the African past that lack such documentation. In short, their historical writing has tended to be text-oriented, whether the text was written or oral, and has shown relatively little interest in the findings of archaeology. Indeed, considering that both Africanist historians and archaeologists have the common task of illuminating the human past in the continent, the inadequate integration of their work is quite remarkable. The explanation for this must surely lie in the very different scholarly traditions of the two disciplines. To put it simply, they do not understand one another.

One reason for this might have been the work of earlier archaeologists, who saw their task as the piecing together of Africa's 'prehistory', thus borrowing a European concept that was unsuited to an African context and leading historians to conclude that this was something outside of their subject area. Furthermore, for a long time the character of African prehistory seemed to justify its separation from African history. This was because it was dominated by studies of stone artefact assemblages and of the hunter-gatherer and early farming societies that had produced them, usually during periods in the remote past. Only gradually did archaeologists in Africa begin to investigate later more complex societies in which historians also had an interest and by then both had become set in their ways. When historians did make use of archaeological evidence, archaeologists often thought that insufficient attention was given to its limitations. When archaeologists made use of historical sources, historians frequently felt that this was done uncritically. Furthermore, although historians were used to conflicting interpretations in their own discipline and could understand that different archaeologists could come to different conclusions from the same data, they were unimpressed by the propensity of some archaeologists to produce explanations for which there seemed very little basis. Add to this the increasing dependence of archaeological research on the natural and physical sciences and the theoretical introspection that has come to characterize archaeology, and it is little wonder that history and archaeology remain only weakly integrated.

A consequence of this is that any attempt at a synthesis of the whole of the African past becomes very difficult. Archaeological scholarship has remained dominated by particularism, often involving minute analysis of evidence that in itself has only limited overall relevance but relatively rarely attempting to fit the jigsaw of results together into a coherent story. The problem has been the lack of an adequate model, with too many archaeologists clinging to the obsolete 3-Age System conceived in Europe almost 200 years ago. Thus the non-specialist reader of much of the literature is likely to become enmeshed in mysterious discussions about the African Middle Stone Age or about the differences between the Early Iron Age and the Later Iron Age in East Africa. To achieve an account of the human past in Africa, a much more flexible approach is needed. In recent years a number of archaeological writers have produced syntheses of parts of the continent and occasionally of the whole of it, in which they have attempted to solve this problem. A frequent theme has been the changing interaction of people with their environment, an approach that does allow both archaeological and historical data to contribute to the story that is built up. With the improved ability to date their evidence that archaeologists now have and a greater understanding of the relationship between material cultures and the societies that produced them, there is a better chance than ever before of explaining the lives of people in particular places at particular times. That, surely, is the story that really matters.

These are some of the issues that lie behind the chapters in this book. An attempt has been made to produce a coherent story of the human past in Africa by stringing together a series of significant episodes. In each case, the interpretive approach adopted has been that which is currently most widely accepted but in many instances there is a variety of alternative explanations of the evidence, which interested readers will want to pursue elsewhere. An attempt has also been made to make use of the widest possible selection of evidence, drawing on many disciplines but maintaining archaeological sources as a central strand. The aim has been to show how Africa's forgotten past is gradually being remembered.

FURTHER READING

The references listed here are only an introduction to the subject of each chapter. They contain further references that will assist the reader who wishes to read more. As far as possible recent publications are listed but, in order to include material with sufficiently broad coverage, in some cases quite old publications have had to be included. Selection has also been influenced by availability and the more obscure material has been avoided. Nevertheless, some of the publications might only be found in a major library. For each chapter, wherever possible, the more generally useful source is listed first.

General

Phillipson, D.W. 1993. *African archaeology*, 2nd edn. Cambridge University Press, Cambridge. (3rd edn due 2004.)

Connah, G. 2001. *African civilizations: an archaeological perspective*, 2nd edn. Cambridge University Press, Cambridge.

Africa: the birthplace of humanity

Klein, R.G. 1999. *The human career: human biological and cultural origins*, 2nd edn. University of Chicago Press, Chicago and London, pp. 1–217.

Andrews, P. and Stringer, C. 1989. *Human evolution: an illustrated guide*. British Museum (Natural History), London. (Also useful for Chapters 2 and 3.)

Stone tools and adaptation: the origins of the genus *Homo*

Klein, R.G. 1999. *The human career: human biological and cultural origins*, 2nd edn. University of Chicago Press, Chicago and London, pp. 217–366.

Isaac, G.L. 1977. *Olorgesailie: archaeological studies of a Middle Pleistocene lake basin in Kenya*. University of Chicago Press, Chicago and London.

Africa's gift to the world: the earliest *Homo sapiens*

Klein, R.G. 1999. *The human career: human biological and cultural origins*, 2nd edn. University of Chicago Press, Chicago and London, pp. 266–493.

Singer, R. and Wymer, J. 1982. *The Middle Stone Age at Klasies River Mouth in South Africa*. University of Chicago Press, Chicago and London.

Living off the land: later hunter-gatherers in Africa

Deacon, H.J. 1976. *Where hunters gathered: a study of Holocene Stone Age people in the Eastern Cape*. South African Archaeological Society, Claremont.

Fagan, B.M. and Van Noten, F.L. 1971. *The hunter-gatherers of Gwisho*. Musée Royal de l'Afrique Centrale, Tervuren, Belgium.

Putting ideas on stone: the rock art of southern Africa

Lewis-Williams, J.D. 1983. *The rock art of southern Africa*. Cambridge University Press, Cambridge.

Vinnicombe, P. 1976. *People of the eland: rock paintings of the Drakensberg Bushmen as a reflection of their life and thought*. University of Natal Press, Pietermaritzburg.

Pictures from a lost world: the rock art of the Sahara

Willcox, A.R. 1984. *The rock art of Africa*. Holmes and Meier, New York, pp. 29–54.

Muzzolini, A. 2000. Livestock in Saharan rock art. In Blench, R.M. and MacDonald, K.C. (eds) *The origins and development of African livestock: archaeology, genetics, linguistics and ethnography*. UCL Press, London, pp. 87–110.

Producing food: early developments in North and West Africa

Blench, R.M. and MacDonald, K.C. (eds) 2000. *The origins and development of African livestock: archaeology, genetics, linguistics and ethnography*. UCL Press, London.

van der Veen, M. (ed.) 1999. *The exploitation of plant resources in ancient Africa*. Kluwer Academic/Plenum Publishers, New York.

Producing food: adaptation in North-East and East Africa

See Blench, R.M. and MacDonald, K.C. (eds) 2000 and van der Veen, M. (ed.) 1999, as previous chapter.

The power of metal: the origins of African iron-working

Woodhouse, J. 1998. Iron in Africa: metal from nowhere. In Connah, G. (ed.) *Transformations in Africa: essays on Africa's later past.* Leicester University Press, London and Washington, pp. 160–185.

Vogel, J.O. (ed.) 2000. *Ancient African metallurgy: the sociocultural context.* AltaMira Press, Walnut Creek, California.

Ancient Egypt: 3000 years of achievement

Baines, J. and Malek, J. 2000. *Cultural atlas of Ancient Egypt.* Revised edition, Checkmark Books, New York.

Davies, V. and Friedman, R. 1998. *Egypt.* British Museum Press, London.

Nubia: a meeting place of different people

Shinnie, P.L. 1996. *Ancient Nubia.* Kegan Paul International, London and New York.

O'Connor, D. 1993. *Ancient Nubia: Egypt's rival in Africa.* The University Museum, University of Pennsylvania, Philadelphia.

Aksum: a trading metropolis on the Ethiopian Plateau

Phillipson, D.W. 1998. *Ancient Ethiopia. Aksum: its antecedents and successors.* British Museum Press, London.

Phillipson, D.W. (ed.) 1997. *The monuments of Aksum: an illustrated account.* Addis Ababa University Press, Addis Ababa, in collaboration with The British Institute in Eastern Africa, London.

Church and state: survival in Ethiopia

Pankhurst, R. 2001. *The Ethiopians: a history.* Blackwell, Oxford.

Buxton, D. 1970. *The Abyssinians.* Thames and Hudson, London.

Opportunity and constraint: the Lake Chad story

Connah, G. 1981. *Three thousand years in Africa: Man and his environment in the Lake Chad region of Nigeria.* Cambridge University Press, Cambridge.

Breunig, P., Neumann, K. and Van Neer, W. 1996. New research on the Holocene settlement and environment of the Chad Basin in Nigeria. *African Archaeological Review* 13(2): 111–145.

Facing the Mediterranean: Carthaginian, Greek and Roman North Africa

Manton, E.L. 1988. *Roman North Africa.* Seaby, London.

Hurst, H. 1979. Excavations at Carthage 1977–8: fourth interim report. *The Antiquaries Journal* 59(1): 19–49.

Qsar es-Seghir: front door to Europe, front door to Africa

Redman, C.L. 1986. *Qsar es-Seghir: an archaeological view of medieval life.* Academic Press, Orlando, Florida.

Redman, C.L. 1983. Comparative urbanism in the Islamic Far West. *World Archaeology* 14(3): 355–377.

Jenné-jeno: an early city on the Middle Niger

McIntosh, R.J. 1998. *The peoples of the Middle Niger: the Island of Gold.* Blackwell, Oxford.

McIntosh, S.K. and McIntosh, R.J. 1993. Cities without citadels: understanding urban origins along the middle Niger. In Shaw, T., Sinclair, P., Andah, B. and Okpoko, A. (eds) *The archaeology of Africa: food, metals and towns.* Routledge, London and New York, pp. 622–641.

Voyages in the Sahara: the desert trade with West Africa

Bovill, E.W. 1958. *The golden trade of the Moors.* Oxford University Press, London.

Bulliet, R.W. 1975. *The camel and the wheel.* Harvard University Press, Cambridge, Massachusetts.

Igbo-Ukwu: a challenge from the past

Shaw, T. 1977. *Unearthing Igbo-Ukwu: archaeological discoveries in eastern Nigeria.* Oxford University Press, Ibadan.

Shaw, T. 1978. *Nigeria: its archaeology and early history.* Thames and Hudson, London, pp. 99–124.

Ancestral faces: ancient sculpture in Nigeria

Willett, F. 1967. *Ife in the history of West African sculpture.* Thames and Hudson, London.

Garlake, P. 2002. *Early art and architecture of Africa.* Oxford University Press, Oxford, pp. 109–112, 120–139.

Benin City: from forest power to world fame

Connah, G. 1975. *The archaeology of Benin*. Oxford University Press, Oxford.
Dark, P.J.C. 1973. *An introduction to Benin art and technology*. Oxford University Press, Oxford.

Pots and people: early farmers south of the Equator

Phillipson, D.W. 1977. The spread of the Bantu language. *Scientific American* 236(4): 106–114.
Vansina, J. 1995. A slow revolution: farming in subequatorial Africa. *Azania* 29–30: 15–26.

The testimony of the dead: life in the Upemba Depression

de Maret, P. 1982. The Iron Age in the west and south. In Van Noten, F. (ed.) *The archaeology of Central Africa*. Akademische Druck- und Verlagsanstalt, Graz, Austria, pp. 77–96 (see pp. 87–95).
de Maret, P. 1997. Savanna states (section on The Luba Kingdom). In Vogel, J.O. (ed.) *Encyclopedia of precolonial Africa: archaeology, history, languages, cultures, and environments*. AltaMira Press, Walnut Creek, California, pp. 498–501.

'One beautiful garden': production and power amongst the Great Lakes

Reid, A. 1997. Lacustrine states. In Vogel, J.O. (ed.) *Encyclopedia of precolonial Africa: archaeology, history, languages, cultures, and environments*. AltaMira Press, Walnut Creek, California, pp. 501–507.
Connah, G. 1996. *Kibiro: the salt of Bunyoro, past and present*. British Institute in Eastern Africa, Memoir 13, London.

Facing two worlds: the trading settlements of the East African coast

Horton, M. and Middleton, J. 2000. *The Swahili: the social landscape of a mercantile society*. Blackwell, Oxford.
Horton, M. 1987. The Swahili Corridor. *Scientific American* 257(3): 76–84.

Projecting power: Great Zimbabwe and related sites

Pikirayi, I. 2001. *The Zimbabwe Culture: origins and decline in southern Zambezian states*. AltaMira Press, Walnut Creek, California.
Garlake, P. 1973. *Great Zimbabwe*. Thames and Hudson, London.

Deserted settlements with a story: later farmers in southern Africa

Mitchell, P. 2002. *The archaeology of southern Africa*. Cambridge University Press, Cambridge. Chapter 12: Later farming communities in southernmost Africa.

Maggs, T. 1976. Iron Age patterns and Sotho history on the southern Highveld: South Africa. *World Archaeology* 7(3): 318–332.

Outsiders on the inside: the impact of European expansion

Posnansky, M. and DeCorse, C.R. 1986. Historical archaeology in Sub-Saharan Africa – a review. *Historical Archaeology* 20(1): 1–14.

Mitchell, P. 2002. *The archaeology of southern Africa*. Cambridge University Press, Cambridge. Chapter 13: The archaeology of colonialism.

Remembering Africa's past

Connah, G. 1998. Static image: dynamic reality. In Connah, G. (ed.) *Transformations in Africa: essays on Africa's later past.* Leicester University Press, London and Washington, pp. 1–13.

Robertshaw, P. 2000. Sibling rivalry? The interaction of archeology and history. *History in Africa* 27: 261–286.

INDEX